RECOLLECTIONS

LIST OF WORKS
BY
FRANK T. BULLEN

THE CRUISE OF THE "CACHALOT"

IDYLLS OF THE SEA

THE LOG OF A SEA WAIF

WITH CHRIST AT SEA

THE MEN OF THE MERCHANT
SERVICE

A SACK OF SHAKINGS

A WHALEMAN'S WIFE

DEEP-SEA PLUNDERINGS

THE APOSTLES OF THE SOUTH-EAST

SEA WRACK

SEA PURITANS

SEA SPRAY

CREATURES OF THE SEA

BACK TO SUNNY SEAS

A SON OF THE SEA

ADVANCE AUSTRALASIA

FRANK BROWN, SEA APPRENTICE

A BOUNTY BOY

THE CALL OF THE DEEP

THE PIRATE HUNTERS

TOLD IN THE DOG WATCHES

THE BITTER SOUTH

BEYOND

CUT OFF FROM THE WORLD

THE SEED OF THE RIGHTEOUS

FIGHTING THE ICEBERGS

A COMPLEAT SEA COOK

FROM WHEEL AND LOOK-OUT

THE SALVAGE OF A SAILOR

THE CONFESSIONS OF A TRADESMAN

&c. &c.

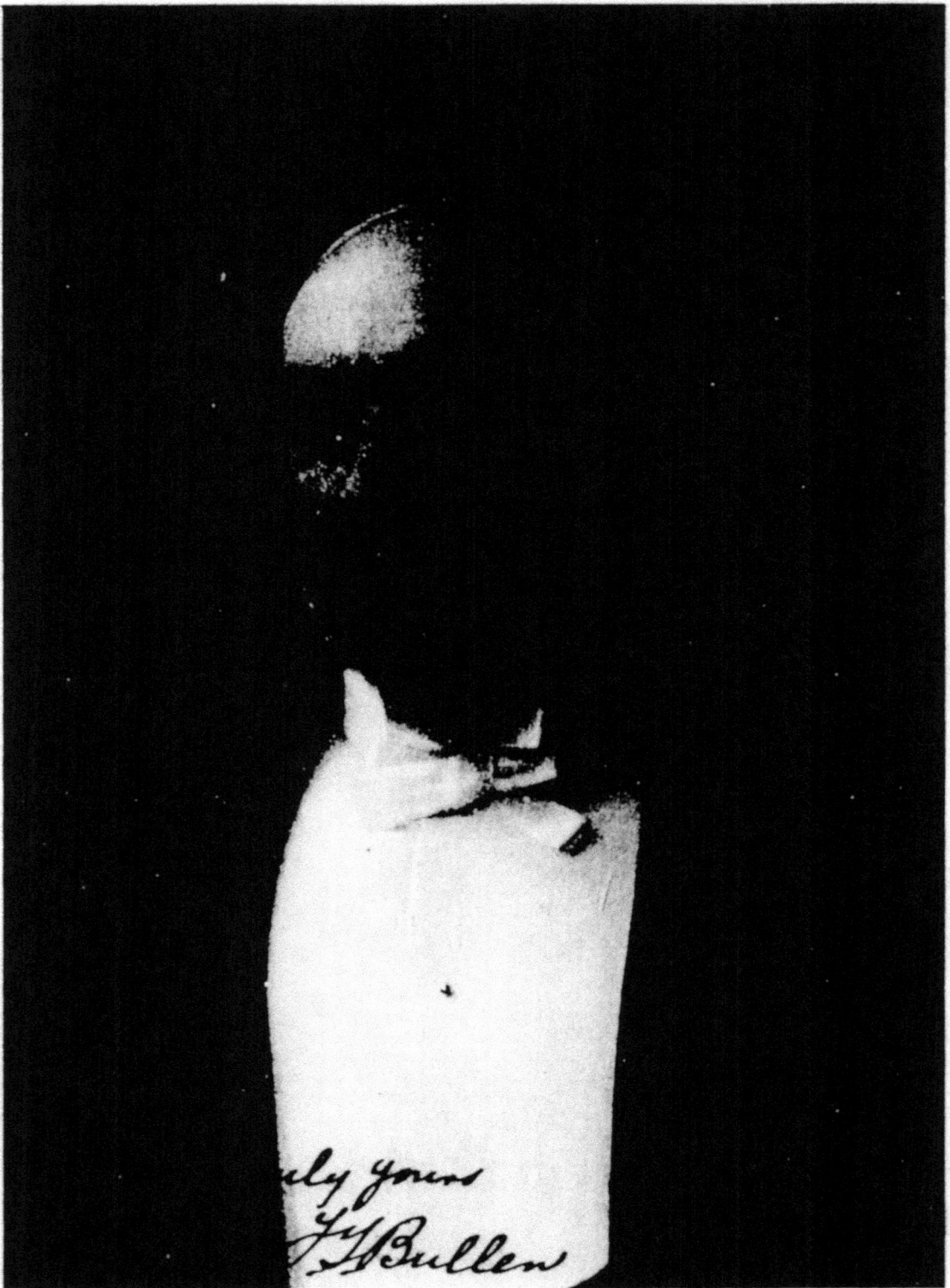

uly yours
FBullen

Vandyk ph.

RECOLLECTIONS

THE REMINISCENCES OF THE BUSY LIFE OF
ONE WHO HAS PLAYED THE VARIED PARTS
OF SAILOR, AUTHOR & LECTURER

BY

FRANK T. BULLEN

AUTHOR OF "THE CRUISE OF THE 'CACHALOT,'" &c.

WITH PORTRAIT

LONDON
SEELEY, SERVICE & CO. LIMITED
38 GREAT RUSSELL STREET
1915

CONTENTS

CHAPTER   PAGE

        INTRODUCTION 11

    I. MY EARLIEST RECOLLECTIONS . . . 19

   II. RANDOM MEMORIES 33

  III. MY FIRST LECTURES 51

  IV. THE LECTURE TOUR 63

   V. THE REAL BEGINNING 75

  VI. SCOTLAND 89

 VII. JOURNEYS 103

VIII. HOSPITALITY 121

  IX. HOSPITALITY (continued) . . . 137

   X. HOTELS 147

  XI. CHAIRMEN 163

 XII. CHAIRMEN (continued) 181

XIII. LANTERNISTS 195

XIV. AUDIENCES 211

 XV. AUSTRALASIA 227

XVI. SECRETARIES 241

XVII. DISCURSIONS 257

XVIII. DIVAGATIONS 275

XIX. ART OR APTITUDE 291

 XX. SUMMING UP 305

INTRODUCTION

IT may very well be that I am doing something now which is totally unnecessary, indeed that is a foregone conclusion as far as many omnivorous readers are concerned, for they never by any chance read a Preface or an Introduction. But only the other day I was reading an interesting volume of reminiscences, and the writer said that after the publisher had received the manuscript he wrote sternly demanding the reason why there was no Introduction. More, he said that one must be written forthwith, and it was so.

Now I cannot honestly say that I, like that writer whom I have quoted, am a novice at book writing, or have much to learn concerning the ways of publishers, since this book will make about the thirty-sixth that has been perpetrated by me during the last seventeen years. Too many, far too many, I know (this to forestall the obvious remark), but what I want to say is that in no case have I ever been asked for an Introduction, or questioned why I had written one. Follows inevitably the remark,

"Why this one, then? Can't you let your book tell its own tale?"

And yet I feel very strongly that an Introduction to this book is needed, if ever a book needed such a thing. For I really believe that it may be my last; I dare not be more definite than that, though I would dearly love to emulate those giants of literature who can calmly announce that they have written their last page for publication, that for good or ill their message has been delivered and they will say no more. Ah no, fate has not dealt kindly enough with me for that, and because the snarl of the proverbial wolf is never out of my ears and the spoor of his stealthy footfall is but too clearly traceable near my door, I must still be ready to take up my pen. This Introduction may serve as my valedictory, if, as it is most reasonable to expect, this book happens to be my last.

And now for the Introduction. For a good many years I have been telling the stories that I have gathered here. It may very well be, of course, that, as Kipling says, all that seemed so definite and amusing in the spoken word has escaped when committed to paper. But I hope not, because I have often been asked why I did not write my reminiscences of the lecture platform, and I have always made some excuse, so that now when I have done it at last, it would be a great pity for it to be a failure.

Of course, the thing has been done before ; it would be strange if it hadn't ; but I have not had the pleasure of reading even the very entertaining book written on the subject by the late Paul Blouet (Max O'Rell), a veritable prince of humorists. I am inclined to think that in one sense at any rate this is an advantage in that I cannot consciously or unconsciously have copied any of their sayings, or told of any of their doings, however interesting or funny. For the same reason there cannot be any " chestnuts " in this book. Everything told in it, except where the contrary has been expressly stated, is an experience of my own. I am rather pleased about this, for I have recently been more than a little disgusted to find how many oft-told stories have been repeated in costly books of memoirs, the names of whose writers should have been guarantee enough that they had sufficient good stories of their own to tell without drawing upon antiquities.

I hope I shall be given due credit for the fact that many really good stories (as I think) have been omitted by me simply because the point of them demanded that the actors should be known, and I would not give those good people pain. Other stories I have had to leave out because I was not looking for trouble and because I was somewhat doubtful of the far-reaching operations of the law of libel. And that, I think, is all I can say by way of Introduction to my book.

FRANK T. BULLEN.

BOURNEMOUTH,
Dec. 17, 1914.

PUBLISHER'S NOTE

SINCE these pages were printed Mr. Bullen has passed away. He had been in a precarious state of health for some years, and he himself was well aware that the end might come at any time.

He died at Madeira on February 26th, 1915, in his fifty-seventh year.

March 4, 1915.

CHAPTER I

MY EARLIEST RECOLLECTIONS

CHAPTER I

MY EARLIEST RECOLLECTIONS

A FEW years ago I was in the breakfast-room of the beautiful Hotel Frontenac at Quebec awaiting my meal at a sunny table, when I caught sight of the head waiter. He was so strikingly like the comedian W. H. Berry, to whom I can never be sufficiently grateful for his mirth-compelling performances, that I sent a waiter to request his attendance. He came on the instant, and I immediately asked him if he were any relation to Mr. Berry, although as I could not then recall that gentleman's name, it took me some time to explain whom I meant. Smilingly the head waiter disclaimed the relationship, saying :

" There was never an actor in our family that I know of. I come from a suburb of London called Paddington." (" So do I," I interjected.) " I was born in a little turning off Jonson Place, Harrow Road, called Alfred Road." (" So was I," I interrupted again.) " At number —." " Ah," I said, " my number was next door."

Why this chronicling of the smallest of small beer ? Because I have never seen anybody more delighted than that bright and able man at meeting some one who was born in the same street as himself. We have no choice in the matter, but I doubt very much whether any tie draws men tighter when they meet abroad than that their place of birth was near each other—even in the same town is often enough to set up a friendship almost masonic in its intensity. Wherefore I recall the fact that I first saw the light in that poor street off Jonson Place, but have no recollection of its amenities. For before even I, precocious as I undoubtedly was, grew old enough to know intelligently, or say at eighteen months old, my father and mother quarrelled, the weaker vessel was thrown out, and myself, as well as an elder sister of whom I know nothing except that she did exist, were consigned to the care of a maiden aunt by my father, with a promise, never redeemed, to pay something towards the expense of keeping us.

That shadowy sister very wisely took the earliest opportunity of becoming a shade, so I remember nothing of her but what I have been told. I may say here that I have often, in the terrible years since, had occasion to wish that I too might then have saved myself all further trouble; but alas! a tenacious-ness of purpose and a stock of vitality which has not yet all gone have so far hindered me that, although I am physically a very wreck and was twelve years ago given at the outside three years to live, I am still topside. Well, as a cynical American friend once told me, " That's only one more mistake you've made, I guess." I cannot contradict him.

Thus it came about that my earliest recollections centre on a quaint little house, No. 15 Desboro' Terrace, now called Marlborough Street. By careful comparison and enquiry I have no doubt that I do remember as far back as 1859–60, when I would be 2½ years old. At the end of Desboro' Terrace, remote from the Harrow Road, ran the main line of the Great Western Railway, and turning sharply to the right when you had reached the blank wall that closed the terrace, you came into a row of little houses called Desboro' Place which fronted the line and were only divided therefrom by a narrow roadway and a line of tall rails. My aunt kept a maid—not, God knows, because she had any pride of that sort, but because she was a dressmaker and could not do the housework and attend to her business too, and also, I am ashamed to say, because she usually had some of her brothers sponging upon her. How well I remember once saying to her :

" Auntie, you used to have quite a lot of people to dinner. I can remember Grandfather, Uncle John, Uncle George, Uncle Tom, Uncle Ted, and Aunt Kitty."

" Ah," she replied, " yes, but you never knew that my poor fingers were working for them all, except Aunt Kitty—she always worked hard enough for her keep."

So I said no more. And now I must return to one of my earliest recollections. The maid, her work done, was permitted to take me out, and she used to take me down Desboro' Place and stand me on the coping clutching the rails and looking down at the puff-puffs. There I saw the wonderful engines of that day, the " Charles Dickens," the " Robin Hood," and once the Queen's special engine, the stately " Lord of the Isles," with the big gilt crown on the front. I knew the names of many engines and never wanted to go and see the shops, the puff-puffs supplied all my needs, until one day, in an evil moment for her, she took me over the little wooden foot-bridge that still spans the line there. And a passing engine sent a cloud of steam up through the crevices of the planks of the bridge floor, passing up my little bare legs even unto my waist under my frock. The sensation was a novel one, and thenceforward I clamoured to be led thither. I did not know nor did I care if she, my guardian, approved of it. I have since felt that I might have been exacting, but peace be unto her whoever she was, she never made complaint that I heard of.

Up till last year I often made journeys from Paddington, but never without glancing up at the railings as we passed Desboro' Place (if that is what it is called now) and at once recalling those dim days. They seem to belong to another life, but they had a quiet charm all their own, entirely due to the good influence of my poor aunt, who, amidst all her worries, always kept a cosy corner for me. My education was her chief care, and happily for me we lived next door to a dame-school kept by three maiden ladies. Of my experiences there I have told at length elsewhere, so I will only say here that my principal recollection of next door is of the ladies' father, a nasty old man whose chief delight seemed to be to get me on his knee in the summer-house and puff strong tobacco smoke in my face. It was of no use struggling or screaming, though I did both, he seemed to have no mercy. I was taught by those gentle ladies that it was a deadly sin to hate anybody, but I came as near hating that old man as made very little odds.

Another curious fact emerges about this time when I would be between four and five years old. I could read—indeed I do not know when I learned, so easy did reading always seem—and from the kind of books to the reading of which I was confined, I had a large and extensive vocabulary, the use of which at inopportune moments often made some of my uncles very angry and brought down upon my head many sarcastic comments. But having no one to whom I could talk or play, I used to march in stately fashion round the small garden, holding the grand old Tom cat's tail, as he paced majestically before me, and declaim as if to gaping congregations my addresses upon—ah, I don't remember what! Of course, the themes were religious, could hardly be otherwise remembering my reading, but I would like to know what I used to say aloud then, and the neighbours' opinions thereupon. As I never heard the latter I must assume that I did not make much noise, not even when, as it were, smitten by sudden madness, I varied my sermons with yells of Murder ! Fire ! Thieves ! No, it could not have been noisy, because I remember that it never scared old Dick, the faithful cat. He was my constant companion, so by that I know that I can never have been cruel.

Indeed the whole environment was as pure and cloistered as could be imagined. A worse preparation for a rough-and-tumble with the world could hardly be imagined, but my poor auntie did her best, the best she knew for me, and kept me, as far as in her lay, unspotted from the world. Of course there were, there always must be, occasions when the primitive man comes to the surface, and I was no exception to the rule. As, for instance, we once had visitors and I was ousted from my aunt's bed where I had always slept and put with a Mrs. Rawlins, a large lady whom I had taken a vivid dislike to, for no reason, very early in her visit. To please this person the sheets were taken off and my tender skin was excoriated by the coarse blankets. And she wasn't a nice person. She took up most of the bed; she snored astoundingly, and—well, it doesn't matter now—but I did not sleep a wink all night, and at the earliest opportunity besought my auntie not to let me sleep with that old woman any more. I don't know what was done, but I do know that I was restored to my auntie's bed the next night and said my prayers twice through in sheer gratitude for the relief.

There was a wedding at our house; my Aunt Kitty was married and my prospective uncle endeavoured to ingratiate himself with me. To no purpose. I didn't like him, and I wouldn't be cajoled by him. I was not a bit surprised to find in later years that all my childish aversions were justified. But of that great upheaval one fact stands saliently forward: I had a new muslin Garibaldi with bishops' sleeves and round pearl buttons, a bright plaid skirt, strap shoes and white socks. I was then nearly six years old, but nobody so much as dreamed of a masculine dress for me, and certainly I thought nothing of the matter. But shortly after the wedding at Holy Trinity Church, Paddington, the child of one of my uncles needed baptism, and my wedding garments being fresh, it was deemed a good opportunity for me to be baptised too. Some doubt existed as to whether I had ever been baptised at all, but my poor mother was a Catholic, and I have since learned that, however low she may have sunk, the priest would have insisted upon her child being baptised in the Faith.

Auntie did not know that; she belonged, as she put it, to the " Angelical " Church of England, and so I was baptised at Holy Trinity Church with my infant cousin, and very well do I remember the whole scene. The great empty echoing church and the little group of godfathers and godmothers, the nervous young curate whose cool hand shook so as he placed it on my head and made the sign on my forehead, the clumsy, blundering way in which everybody seemed to behave, except the baby who squalled lustily in the curate's arms and made him go crimson —ah yes—it is all so vividly present to me now. As is also the astounding thought in my small brain that I could do the whole thing so much better than any of them, conscious, mind you, that I was the most self-possessed person in the little crowd. And that night, when as usual I mounted to the top of the house and went to bed alone, for auntie did not come till one a.m. sometimes, I felt singularly defiant as I knelt to say my prayers. The hole in the palliasses made by their being turned end for end, as sailors say, and the corners cut out for the bedposts coming together, quite lost their power to frighten me by the possibility of some evil thing coming out and doing me some mysterious harm ; nor did I any longer fear old Joe, Miss Moore's great macaw, with which she used to threaten us when we were naughty, though he had hitherto always seemed to be lurking under the bed every night.

No ; like the 'Badian and Jamaican nigger who considers that going to church on the occasion of his marriage (though there is often a long family by that time) gives him a clean bill of spiritual health for all past and future soul-sicknesses, I had some dim idea that from henceforth I was immune from the terror that walketh by night. I did not put it that way, of course, but that certainly was the immediate effect of my baptism. But it was a clean little soul, after all. Lack of opportunity had prevented sin, and I did not even know the joy of an occasional theft of jam or sugar. Then came an episode which I am sure most people will find difficult of belief, and no one more so than myself, for a reason presently to be given.

One of my uncles was a gentleman's groom, and through lying in a damp bed he had contracted some disease of the throat which made him an invalid for five long years. All that time he lived with auntie, but I believe his sweetheart, who was lady's maid at the big house where he had been employed, remained faithful to him and paid auntie for his keep. He attended Dr. Sieveking at St. Mary's Hospital, and always took me with him on the days when he went. My recollections of those days are all grey. He never joked, never even talked to me, and as for giving me a penn'orth of sweets—I doubt if the idea ever occurred to him. At last he died; and I, who did not know anything about death, of course was banished from all the discussions which took place. Of course, being a secretive and very quiet child, I asked no questions; but I bided my time. It came. He was laid in his coffin in the next room to ours—the bedroom which auntie and I occupied.

They sent me up to bed as usual and I went through all the usual formulæ of retiring. And then I got up, crept out upon the landing, listened intently, and, hearing nothing, fled into the death room. There lay the coffin on its trestles covered with a sheet. The moon shone through the white blinds as if they had not been there. I drew the sheet back and looked upon that face. I do not believe I should have been terrified at all, but a handkerchief was tied under his jaw and over his head and it gave him an appearance that I cannot describe. And one of his eyes was half open. I drew the sheet rapidly back, I slid to the door, passed through it, closed it behind me, listened again—no sound—crept into bed and covered my head with the bedclothes. I lay for over an hour with thumping heart and panting breath, but I slept at last. And I have never been able to look upon the dead without terrible sensations since —indeed, I have not seen a dead face since I lost my youngest boy fifteen years ago.

But I notice that I am lingering too long over those earliest days. Yet I must just pause a moment over the change from my much-loved and comfortable petticoats to trousers. My poor old grandfather had died and been buried by my auntie, and from a

pair of his best trousers she made me my initial pair.
Poor lady, she knew rather less than most people of
the make of masculine garments, but she did her best,
and presently, in the midst of a little group of giggling
work-girls I was endued with the tubes. That's
what they were, just tubes, and my little legs felt as
forlorn and distant in them as if they had no connection with me. I draw a veil over other details as
not being seemly, but as I forlornly surveyed myself
standing there, with those tubes nearly reaching to
my shoulders, the giggling of the girls burst into
unquenchable laughter and I nearly died with shame.
No child likes to be an object of laughter; but that
I certainly was then, and all my aunt's well-meant
efforts to stay the yells of laughter were fruitless.

They were taken off me then, but I wore them;
oh yes, I wore them, and what I endured from the
street urchins who saw me in them I can never tell—
the trouble was too great. But as all those troubles
were soon to be merged in a much greater trouble, I
must pass them over and get on. Once and once
only I had seen my mother. A heap of old clothing
like a pile of autumn leaves was shown me, and I was
told that *that* was my mother who had come to see
me but had been taken ill. I was frightened, and ran
to hide myself. And I never saw her again. It was
not long after this that my poor auntie died, and I
having no one, for my father being a British workman with a strong desire to back horses and play

billiards, could not be expected to want me, I was flung upon the streets.

I have told the story of that time fairly fully in different books, but I may perhaps just pause here to point out that the position was not common. For I had been brought up in a sheltered home without even the faintest knowledge of evil, brought up more like a tender little girl than a boy, and then suddenly, at the age of nine, I was flung into a veritable maelstrom of vice. I don't comment upon this; I just state the fact that this happened in 1866, when I was barely nine years old.

CHAPTER II

RANDOM MEMORIES

CHAPTER II

RANDOM MEMORIES

SO very minutely have I detailed in four different books the various happenings in my life that I am confined to two periods for recollections, but those two embrace what to me at any rate were full of interest. The first of these was my officer time at sea, and the second the period since my emancipation from the desk until now. It is true that I have touched upon events in the first period in *With Christ at Sea*, but very lightly, and there are many reminiscences unconnected with that book which rush to the mind now.

For instance, there is a little matter connected with my visit to Noumea, New Caledonia, when I was mate of a colonial barque, that for some queer reason has been persistent in my memory lately. I'm sure I wonder that I haven't used it before, for it has all the elements of a good story in it. It must be remembered that Noumea is a French convict settlement, and while I say nothing about the treatment of the convicts, I need not labour the point that any attempt to escape means the shortest possible shrift to the escapee if caught in the act. Now at the time of which I write there were five warships in the harbour, a few schooners, my own barque, and a French convict ship. I had been ashore and found on coming down to the beach that I had, as we say, " lost my passage," i.e. my boat had gone without me.

Now I had a great dread of staying ashore at night in a foreign port (oh, yes, I know that proves me to have been any opprobrious sort of thing you like, but we'll take that as read), and so it never even occurred to me to go back to the hotel—at least that's what they called it. Nor did I dare to shout, for though the night was still we were a long way out, and I was afraid of bringing the gendarmes down upon me. But in the clear darkness I saw about a dozen boats moored some hundred feet or so off the beach, and without thinking I waded in and swam off to the nearest one. She was fastened at the bows by a chain passing through a ring in the stern inside, and I started to unreeve that chain. How many fathoms of it I hauled up I can't imagine, or why the rattle of it didn't rouse all Noumea ; but I came to the end at last, and it wouldn't pass the ring.

Obviously I had hauled in the wrong end; and the whole dreary, noisy process had to be reversed ; but after hours of labour I got that big boat adrift, and aroused nobody. She was down by the head with the weight of chain, and there was much water in her, but the chief fact evident to me when I got fairly adrift was that there were no oars! I hadn't thought of that before. So I got a bottom board and did the best I could with that in the direction I supposed my ship to lie. Presently a shadowy hulk loomed up ahead and a hoarse *Qui va là?* greeted me. Need I say that I did not reply. But I sweated hugely, expecting every moment to be shot. Three ships I passed, the sentry hailing me like that, and never an answer from me. And then, with the nyctalopic eyesight of the sailor, I saw my ship ahead. I forgot the feeble tides of the South Seas, and worked like a beaver to gain the gangway. I did, and (I have grieved over the act ever since, but what was I to do?) sent the boat adrift as I triumphantly climbed the side ladder and sought my bunk. I have only to add that no echo of that night's exploit ever reached me, and I had to come to the conclusion that the occasional escapes of convicts was comparatively easy when the escapees were prepared to risk their lives in the operation.

Another adventure which was good to laugh at afterwards but very unpleasant at the time befell me on the beach at Tamatave, Madagascar. I was mate of a pretty little brig and went ashore one night to fetch the captain, who was dining with somebody. It was a glorious night with a full moon, but very late, and I do not know what prompted me to go with the two good fellows who rowed. We were soon ashore and, the time hanging heavily, we all decided on a bathe. A most enjoyable swim and wallow in the tepid water followed, and we emerged to dress in our two garments which lay on the beach near by. But as we came ashore a troop of huge ferocious dogs such as then infested Tamatave suddenly rushed at us, and we made for the first place of refuge that presented itself, a huge pyramid of beef bones which lay near the sea, white under the moon-rays. We fled up that pyramid, shedding blood and bad words at every stumbling stride, but we gained the summit without a dog bite, and from that eminence turned on our foes and bombarded them with bones.

It was very cold to our naked bodies, and the dogs looked horribly fierce down there, but every now and then we rejoiced to hear a well-aimed shin bone go bang against some mangy hide, and the following yells were music to our ears. Our shying redoubled, and after a few minutes we were able to descend from our captivity and chase the brutes away. We had suffered many things to our bare feet and legs from the jagged bones, but we took those bones on board for cargo, and I often shuddered afterwards to think what our feelings would have been had we then known that every hollow contained a centipede, a scorpion, or a tarantula. Ugh! they furnished our ship for us, those beastly bones, with these lethal vermin, and we had spent nearly a quarter of an hour among that magazine of venom, naked.

Since, while I was mate of that vessel, the fever smote down every member of the ship's company except the bos'un and myself, and we carried on the work of the ship in Zanzibar with slaves, there would reasonably seem to be many opportunities for adventure. And that was certainly the case; but the whole life was so strange and exotic, so full of differences from the ordered life of our civilisation, that I feel it impossible to select from it any salient incidents. Especially as these are recollections, not inventions, and I don't recall any scenes of bloodshed on board. Only I once had the temerity to go ashore on a Sunday at Zanzibar, when a wild mêlée was raging and crowds of naked blacks were yelling at the pitch of their voices while slashing furiously about them with their long butcher knives whose edges were keen as razors.

I afterwards commented upon what I had seen to Ali, our Suahili cook, who immediately waxed enthusiastic upon the joys of the English Sunday, when, as he put it :—

" All mans plenty get dlunk, plenty fight, plenty play knife." Yes, he called it play : with a smile like a huge white gash across his ebony face, he showed me his scars ; my conscience, the fellow must have been cut to ribbons in his time. One particularly ghastly scar he had on his right thigh. It was a whitish knotted lump almost as big as a shut fist I enquired about it, and he nonchalantly informed me that it was got one Sunday morning when the boys were playing.

" And what did you do to the man who gave it you ? "

" Oh, I cut 'im belly orf," with the most careless air.

" What happened to you then ? " I enquired.

" Two year prison ; s'pose kill man, Sultan make work in gaol two year."

That was all, but it will be no matter for surprise that I sequestrated the knives of both Sa'adi and Ali, our cook and steward, as well as a particularly fine dagger belonging to the former. But one of those Sunday morning " plays " must be seen to be believed possible.

And now I must make a long " fleet," as we call it, to a time more understandable by my readers, a time when I began to realise that money might be earned by writing, not, that is, in the service of the Government, but for myself. It was a wonderful discovery, for I made it at a time when I sorely needed a little extra money. Not that I might belong to two or three West End clubs, rent an expensive flat, and entertain folks at restaurants where the bills were of fabulous amounts, but for sheer necessities. That this is no figure of speech may be understood from the fact that I wrote my first stories on my shop counter while waiting for customers. Now I'm not going to ape the usual conventional lie and say, " Ah, but they were happy days ! " They weren't. They were very wretched days, full of trouble and apprehension of trouble, even worse. It may be that the full story of that time will never be told, but I have given as much of it to the world as I could in the *Confessions of a Tradesman*, a book better reviewed than any I have written ; a book about which I have received double the number of eulogistic letters evoked by any other of my books, but which has sold, so my publishers tell me, less than 400 copies, and has now gone out of print.

But I look back to that time with gratitude and joy because of the new kind world to which it gave me entrance. Not all at once, that could hardly be expected, but with far less preliminary than might have been expected. And in spite of all that has been said about the poor rewards of literature as a profession, most of which is, I believe, quite true, I make bold to say that I do not believe there is any other profession where the rewards are so immensely greater than the merit in the majority of cases. There are dozens of writers now eating the fat and drinking the sweet, lying soft and riding swift, who as far as any merit in themselves is concerned, are worth exactly 0. They have caught the public ear, that is all. True there are some, thank God, who have attained a grand income by sheer gigantic merit, but they are few and, alas ! when they have made a fortune it is the most difficult thing in the world to keep it from the clutch of the dishonest company promoter.

But to return. I am grateful to literature because it did for me what no other form of money-getting could do save Charity, which, always hateful, is usually utterly inadequate to the needs. But most of all, it saved me from the Office. Here I must refrain, because otherwise I could fall a-cursing like a very drab when I remember that place and all that I endured there. I was forty-two years of age; I had four children, and I had not a penny at my back; yet such was my horror of the Office and all its works that as soon as I received an offer from a London newspaper of a year's engagement at £2 per week with six months' notice on either side, I joyfully accepted it, and at once resigned the situation I had endured so long. If this be not a measure of my hatred of that place I do not know what is, and yet I am sure that many such employments, though the salary be small, are as pleasant to the workers as any occupation can be in this world. It entirely rests with the superiors (*sic*).

But this is not anecdote, although it certainly is recollection. Now and from henceforth my two avocations ran concurrently, lecturing and writing, and I suppose I worked very hard. Looking back at those years I am inclined to think so; most people who knew me and what I was doing seemed to think so too; but I, accustomed to the most strenuous physical life and breasting a stormy sea of worry at the same time, felt that it was all play. I think I should have been entirely happy but for the sad fact that I had no home. I was essentially a home-lover, yet I had no home in the true sense of the word. More than that I cannot say, except that one day I awoke to the fact that at last and at great cost I had achieved a home and was about to enjoy life as I had never done before. It is true that I was rapidly nearing my jubilee, and that my health was permanently impaired, but—and oh! what a huge but it is—I had emerged into the sunshine and, though that I could not know, ten years of placid joy lay before me.

I had taken a house in the country about fifty miles from London, an ideal place as I thought, the rent being low, £40 a year, for which I had a good eight-roomed house and nearly two acres of land well laid out as orchard, kitchen garden, flower garden, lawn, and plenty of outbuildings. Oh, it was altogether charming, although I afterwards found that the soil was cold and hungry. But that did not matter to me; I was not farming, and I am not going to say a word in dispraise of the place where I spent ten happy years. I must say, however, that they would not have been so happy but that I gave explicit instructions that none of the village talk was to be told me, nor did I do any visiting whatever. You will say that I must have lived like a hermit. Oh no, I had plenty of visitors from town; I often had to go away myself, so that I did not feel at all isolated, and in any case I could never have endured the venomous, slanderous small talk which is the mental pabulum of most English village folk. Poor people, I can hardly blame them. Talk is their only recreation, and it has been very wisely told us that a " multitude of words wanteth not sin."

However, before I had more than sampled the beauties of the place, and when I had only tasted, as it were, the joys of the " harvest bugs " of summer which made the place almost unbearable, I received an invitation from the Royal Mail Steam Packet Company to be their guest, bringing with me a secretary if I wished, for their West Indian and Central American trip. At first I demurred, for a sea trip has long lost its charms for me; but the offer was enhanced by the promise of a large sum of money if I would write an account of my trip, so I immediately set about finding a secretary. A young lady who did my typing agreed to come, the facilities being so royal, a four-berth cabin each and another cabin for an office, and we sailed from Southampton on what I must always regard as the pleasantest voyage of my life. It is a very long time since I have had any communication with the Royal Mail, and I am never likely to meet Sir Owen Phillips again, therefore I am the more free to say that in the Company's treatment of me and my secretary the adjective I have used above is the only adequate one.

We went all over the loyal island of Barbados, up to the Blue Mountains of Jamaica, up to the capital of Costa Rica, where the climate is of heaven and the death rate was then the highest in the world, for reasons that I may not dwell upon ; all along the line of the Panama Canal from Colon to Panama and back, from La Guayra to Caracas, President Castro's stronghold, and to the pearl fisheries of Margharita Porlomar. Yes, you may say, but surely you must have had many adventures during such a trip as that. True, we did ; and I have recorded them all in a book now out of print, I believe, called *Back to Sunny Seas*. The fine flavour of it all is there, but sitting here in the sunny evenings I often think of those halcyon days and smile, a pleasant happy smile, there was so little that called for anything but happiness.

And yet, in pursuance of Pope's profound maxim that " Man never is, but always to be, blest," I often yearned for home and wondered, wondered how things were going there. And when at last, after nearly four months' joy, we sighted Plymouth one morning at dawn, I could only point and use my handkerchief, for the dear land ahead took away from me the power of speech. It was so when I was a child on my first return to England—see *The Log of a Sea Waif* (*passim*)—and it has grown with the years. It was so good to get home again. It had been very good to visit those strange exotic countries *en prince*, very good to give much simple pleasure to another; but I have always felt and always shall feel, I suppose, that the chief, the choicest charm of a holiday is returning. I think that is how it ought to be. It may be necessary to go, but it should be most delightful to return.

And, as should be the case, all had been well during my absence. Nothing untoward had happened. So that I could sit down now to the finishing of the book with a light heart, with the lecturing season still some months ahead. Happy! happiness had only just come to me, and I felt full of it. I had realised before that such fullness of life as was vouch-safed to other men, though they did not seem to appreciate it as I thought they should, was not for me, and upon the principle of the Spanish proverb, " The best thing to do when it is raining, is to let it rain ! " I had " let on " to be content. But my word, the true test of contentment, I am sure, is that the contentee won't change his condition. And I had never been in such a position. Now, however, I felt that all was so well with me that it could never be better. That I was blest above, far, far above my deserts. All that had ever gone before was just drivel compared with the large joy that was now mine.

And thinking of those happy days, coming as they

did after so much storm and stress, I still hold the same opinion. I know that many wise folk with their flats in town and their nightly symposia at the club will sneer at me, but let them. I was getting closely on for fifty and I had never known joy; now it lay all about me, and though my income was never very much, I had the priceless reputation in the village of " the gen'l'man as allus pays everybody soon's they asks him." My heavenly Father, I would rather that were engraved upon my tomb than that I had commanded troops that conquered half the world.

My friends knew where to come, and they always found open house, they never wore out their welcome. How could they ? I had known the want of welcome, they never should. And I know to-day that none of them that are alive will refuse me the meed of being a hospitable fellow, nor did I do my hospitality at any poor tradesman's expense.

I have said that the soil was a cold and hungry one. Well, so it was, and my old gardener toiled over it in vain very often ; but it did produce many things, and especially did it bring forth the two things I liked best in the way of eatables—green peas and new potatoes. Food as a rule is to me an appalling nuisance. I don't know which is worse, taking it in or the process of assimilation, but I must make an exception in favour of green peas and new potatoes and mint. And these we had at Millfield in such profusion as I have never seen before or since. True, I paid top price for seed, true, I spared nothing in their production, but here in Bournemouth to-day I must needs pay more directly, and never, no never get anything like the satisfaction that I did then. Oh ye fat and greasy citizens, know ye the joy of gathering green peas that ye have watched from the germination ? Know ye the delight of *shelling* them and of passing them into the kitchen (with appropriate comments anent the cooking), and then the supreme joy of digging the spoon down deep in the piled-up dish and ladling them out to your chums with much dish gravy—not hot water ? Then you know nothing at all of the joy of the table ; and as for the Frenchman and his *petits pois* and butter, etc., bah! I've no patience, he doesn't know anything about it. I speak an alien tongue to him.

But the garden was a perennial delight. I could not do any gardening, I couldn't stoop, though of the thinnest, because my constitutional ailment of the lungs wouldn't let me, but I was death on superintending; also I loved to patrol the garden and the hedges before breakfast in the morning and watch the birds at their work, as well as the little things growing. Oh yes, I have no pretensions to scholarship; I cannot express myself like the late R.L.S., but I did enjoy that most blessed time. And when I come to die I hope I shall remember it just as well, for indeed we should all think gratefully of the happiest time in our lives. If I wanted to fill many pages

I could easily do so with happenings down there that have never been noted before—how could they ? I dare say the village annals contain them, but they are not published, thank God—none of my friends have written them down—they were too happy to do more than enjoy. And if they ever missed me, and they sometimes did when an article was due, one of them would say, " Oh, he's gone to write another novel, don't disturb him. Let's have another." And so the happy hours wore on.

But now I come to the point when I must confine myself more strictly to the lecture reminiscences and leave my beloved Millfield for a while. Though I would have you remember that every return was but a renewal of ancient delights.

CHAPTER III

MY FIRST LECTURES

CHAPTER III

MY FIRST LECTURES

PERHAPS this heading is not strictly accurate, and I should go back another dozen years to the time when in response to an irresistible call I first opened my mouth to speak in public. It was a memorable occasion too. I lived in one basement room in Hazlewood Crescent, Kensal New Town—I beg its pardon, Upper Westbourne Park—and sitting one evening by my first baby's cradle reading, my wife being absent on an errand, a large piece of granite crashed through the window and fell in the cradle. I was full of energy in those days, and although I had no boots on I rushed out and up the area steps into the street in time to see the young miscreant who had flung the stone scampering off. Of course I caught him, I went like the wind, and equally of course I landed one soul-satisfying clout on his head which sent him sprawling across the road and into the kennel opposite.

It was enough, and I returned, panting but quite happy, to forget the incident. The next evening at the corner of the Crescent I made my debut as a member of an open-air band of preachers and was duly called upon to testify. My knees knocked together, my mouth seemed filled with dust, and when I did get a word or two out I did not know my own voice. But I had a kindly tolerant audience, such as I am grateful to say I have ever found, and I was beginning to gain confidence when a grimy urchin, squeezing through the ring of listeners, gave one searching glance at me and yelled to some unseen comrade:

"D'yer, Bill, that's the bloke wot clouted my ear lars' night."

A great burst of laughter went up and I retired, feeling as if sudden annihilation would be a great boon. I wonder now why I was not entirely discouraged, but I only know that from that time forward my appetite for open-air speaking grew until it was a passion with me, and, had I known, became a splendid preparation for the lecture platform. Common gratitude compels me to say here that this practice of speaking in the open air speedily became to me a great and perfect compensation for the sorrows and drawbacks of my daily life. The more so perhaps because I stuck to it in spite of the most effective opposition of all, an opposition which never weakened or failed and embittered the whole of my home life. Yet I never—as far as I know—consciously preached or uttered platitudes in an unctuous voice such as I have often heard and sickened at. I gave my auditors the best I had, the results of extensive and varied reading, common-sense outlook upon life, and a totally unorthodox Christianity. I had a good though untrained singing voice and an excellent memory, so I sang to my audiences, never using a book; I recited chapters of Scripture without the Bible, and had the untellable gratification of seeing masses of men and women, often running into the thousands, swayed by my voice as the wind affects the corn.

Is there any pleasure akin to this? I think not. At any rate, though the above lines may seem somewhat vainglorious, I know that they tell no more than the truth. Had I any doubts about that, the remembrance of the hatred with which I was regarded by many old members of the various open-air bands where I was invited to speak while they stood aside, would reassure me. But I have no doubts. I knew that I was in my proper element and my hearers knew it also.

This brings me naturally to my first lecture. I was associated with a very humble little gathering of Christians at Peckham, a part of whose activities was the providing of free teas periodically during the winter. And it came about that winter befell and there was no money wherewith to purchase any materials for these feeble banquets.

None of the members could help, for we were all living on the edge, and we began to say to ourselves that this year the children must go without. But a new convert was added unto us, filled with the big desire of doing something, and he was mightily distressed at the thought of such a backward stride as we were contemplating. So one evening during a prolonged discussion of ways and means at our little mission hall the thought suddenly occurred to me that if I could get some slides made and we could hire a hall—our own little place not being suitable, I might give a lecture on my experiences in the South Sea Whale Fishery, which ought to bring in something for the Tea Fund. Our new brother seized the notion at once and offered to advance £5 from his savings for the expenses. It was there and then decided to take the Peckham Public Hall for the occasion and when the affair was over, whatever the result, the slides were to be mine to use as I thought fit afterwards.

Everybody worked with a will, and I remember that somebody wrote to Sir John Blundell Maple, because they said as member for the division he was good for a guinea, and he was. I must not forget either that the proprietor of the hall let it to us at half-price and that a lantern enthusiast, Mr. R. Sprules, operated free. Well, the great night came and the hall was crowded. Unhappily here the only hitch occurred at the outset. A highly respected local minister was asked to take the chair, and he, spying a prominent member of his congregation in the audience, said after a few preliminaries:

" Our brother Jones will now lead us in prayer ! "

Remember it was a Public Lecture, composed of all sorts and conditions of men and women, yet that old ass thumped his chair and roared out what would have been blasphemous nonsense if he had known it, for fifteen minutes. Oh dear good patient people, you stood it, or sat it stolidly, but I tremble to think what you might legitimately have done. At last I got started and I can freely confess that my relief at the escape from disaster on that terrible opening was so great as to overcome any stage fright that I might otherwise have felt. The audience was splendid and I grew more and more at my ease with them until I noticed that my slides were nearly finished. Then I had a small panic. Had I given my listeners enough ? Impossible, for I did not seem to have been talking for forty-five minutes. So I leaned forward and asked the time, in a stage whisper, of a friend whom I knew had a watch. He said—his voice wouldn't modulate and filled the hall, " Five past ten, Tom ! "

There was a sudden upheaval, lights were turned up by some wise watcher and half the audience fled to catch trains, for they came from all parts of London. And my superintendent, a genial little chimney-sweep, coming to the front of the platform to " render thanks " cried sobbingly :

" I never knew we 'ad such a bruvver ! "

A few of us adjourned to the local stewed-eel shop for refreshment and mutual congratulations upon the wonderful success of the evening, most wonderful of all in that the net proceeds, after all expenses were paid, came to thirteen pounds, enough to provide, with tea at 1s. a pound, milk at 4d. a tin, and cake at 3d. a pound, refreshment for a noble army of children. Also the fragments were no mean consideration to the parents, as we found later.

But before closing this description of my first lecture I must include one out of the many startling coincidences of my life. Remember this was in Rye Lane in 1896. After the lecture was over a man came up to me and said:

" Mister, I was in one of them whalers you talk about, and I know you have told the truth." And he there and then gave me the most irrefragable proofs of his statement, mentioning names and dates and places which were utterly convincing. But chiefly I was delighted because of the corroboration of my statements, not that I felt they needed such buttressing, but you know what people are. It also established a fact which has since become a commonplace with me, that no matter how remote or unlikely the spot may be, a man who addresses an audience from a public platform is always most liable to have among his hearers some one who can testify to the truth (or falsehood) of his statements from actual personal experience, which should make all lecturers exceedingly careful not to give rein to their imaginative faculties.

This experience, though it launched me as a lecturer, was only profitable in so far as it provided me with slides and a certain understanding of a lecture audience. For although there was thenceforward a considerable demand for my services as a lecturer in the neighbourhood, there was never any pay attached to the business. In fact my good friends all seemed to think that they did me great honour by inviting me and they often carried this idea so far as to resent the mild suggestion, made by my friend the enthusiastic lanternist, that they should pay for the gas which he provided. But he, like myself, was of a cheerful as well as humble disposition and we went on with the work until we found that no effort was ever made to get an audience for us, and so we often addressed ourselves to a mere handful of people in a large chapel. In this connection I may say that one night when I was to lecture at a certain big chapel in Peckham, a stout roughish-looking man strolled in and asked my friend who was getting the lantern ready what was on.

" A lecture on Whales and Whale Fishing," replied my friend.

" Ar," said the enquirer, turning on his heel to go, " s'rimps is more in my line."

It is only true to confess that I was getting seriously discouraged, for it seemed obvious that nobody wanted to hear me even for nothing, while my evangelical oratory was always appreciated. But on the advice of a friend I wrote to Mr. Christy asking if he would put me on his list on the strength of the entertainment I had to offer. Very wisely he demurred as not knowing anything about me, but he promised to see if he could get me any engagements and the result of them would guide his future conduct towards me. Meanwhile Mr. Reginald Smith of Smith, Elder & Co. invited me to give my lecture in his spacious drawing-room, and paid me a good fee. Probably all my hearers on that occasion had read the *Cruise of the Cachalot*, just published by my host, at any rate they were immensely appreciative and I immediately secured two engagements at what I then considered good fees.

This led me directly to the discovery of an old truth that what costs people nothing they do not value. For I found that as my fees rose so did the appreciation I met with increase until I found myself becoming quite a popular lecturer and compelled to raise my fees considerably in order to keep the engagements from overwhelming me. But this did not come for some time, two or three years, in fact. Yet I can honestly say that my efforts, which were a pure delight to me, were received with wonderful enthusiasm and appreciation, and I was always treated as if I were conferring favours instead of receiving them. Perhaps this was due in a great measure to the fact that I loved the business, that as soon as I opened my mouth upon the platform I felt as if the audience and I had known one another for years and I could just tell them confidentially all I knew about the matter in hand without taxing any of them unduly either to hear or to understand me. At any rate I did enjoy myself and I know, without any boasting, that I gave joy to others. And I am sure that the foundation of it all was those long years of open-air speaking and singing, when listeners had to be held by their interest in the speaker or not at all.

CHAPTER IV

THE LECTURE TOUR

CHAPTER IV

THE LECTURE TOUR

MAY I very humbly intimate that in what follows I speak for myself alone, I have no experience whatever of my fellow-lecturers, many of whom I know and admire and love, but am entirely ignorant of their experiences on the platform or on the tour. So that I must beg the reader to remember that what I say may be and very probably is peculiar to myself alone and that other lecturers may have experiences of an entirely different nature.

In what I believe to have been my first public engagement at Glenalmond College, in Perthshire, I was notably handicapped in several ways. I was eager and excited at the honour, as I naturally felt it, but I was very poor both in money and time, so I booked from King's Cross by the midnight train, third class, of course. Our compartment contained five, but one man, who had arrived early, had made himself comfortable with rug and pillow stretched full length upon the seat, and my share of that side was quite cramped. Yet I did not protest or claim that he was taking much more than his share, for I was diffident, inexperienced in railway travelling, and, moreover, of a peaceable disposition. But I spent a miserable night, sleepless, cold and painfully stiff, so that the cup of coffee at Newcastle which I obtained at the refreshment room came as a veritable elixir of life to me.

My seat companion had not wakened, nor did he until arrival in Edinburgh, and I am afraid I looked upon his prostrate form with bitter envy. Oh the bleakness of that dawn along the east coast of Northumberland! It struck a chill into my very soul, and the entry to Edinburgh seemed to sweat that coldness down. For as you all know, in common with most picturesque places, the railway approach to the Athens of the North is as if you were Dante being led by Virgil towards the hopeless Gate. And Waverley Station was in a state of chaos. They were building it and the pitiless sleet poured down upon a vast raffle of rafters and wreckage of every sort. Nevertheless I managed to get some more coffee and a Bap, then got me unto my carriage as a place of refuge from the all-pervading wretchedness of that morning.

We crossed the Forth Bridge in a sleet storm so thick that much as I longed to make the acquaintance of that mighty structure I was only able to catch passing glimpses of the great tubes as we flitted between them. Opening the window was out of the question. So I settled down again until arrival at Perth, where the weather and the general outlook were as bad as ever. I was momentarily cheered by a sign which offered hot baths, for the prospect of one sent a glow all through me. Alas, the price was half a crown and I turned sadly away, wondering mightily why such elementary comforts should be available only for the rich. I owe that bathroom a grudge still, for I am sure that the charge was an abominably extortionate one.

Unfortunately I had arranged with the College authorities to send a conveyance for me to Methven Station in the afternoon, so I had the day before me. And such a day! You ladies and gentlemen who only know Perth in its summer garb can hardly imagine its bleakness to a poor stranger landing in it at 9 a.m. on a December day with only a few shillings and a return ticket to London in his pocket, and obliged to wait somewhere until the afternoon. I draw a veil over the misery of that morning although my experiences were quaint enough, involving as they did, the absorption of a " gless " of hot whisky at a coffee tavern, and the overhearing of some of the strangest sounds from customers who came into the room where I sat, and drank neat whisky with a mouthful of water after it, a fashion I had only seen before in America.

At last I could stand Perth and the sleet no longer and I fled to the station for Methven, arriving there to find, as I thought, a station only in the midst of a wide solitude. But there was Erchie, the old porter factotum, and he was a host in himself. I think he took pity upon the puir Southron bodie, certainly he took interest, for his questions were many and searching. The end of them was that I found myself in a " ma-sheen," in this case a dog-cart, trundling along the road towards Glenalmond, utterly weary and cold and wretched, but buoyed up by the feeling that I was near my journey's end.

It was a long drive in the open, but the sleet had ceased and only the bitter wind searched my none too well clad form. But when we arrived at the College my amazement at the magnificent pile—it must be remembered that I had never *seen* a great Public School before—was so great that I almost forgot my physical discomfort in admiration. Then my hostess enwrapped me in her gentle hospitality, and having heard my brief account of the recent happenings she first gave me hot tea, then ordered me a hot bath, a warm bed, and laid upon me strict injunction not to appear until dinner-time. Now it is true that I had never been so received in my life before and that perhaps would account for the vivid impression it made upon my memory, but the thoughtful care of it all coming as and when it did would suffice to have made that first visit to Mrs. Skrine's hospitable roof memorable.

I emerged at dinner-time from that luxurious bed a new man, feeling fit for any fate, and the rest of my visit there—I stayed the week-end—was sheer delight, for it was like a first glimpse of a new world. So that when my "masheen" came at 7.30 on Monday morning to take me to the station I faced the long bitter drive with the greatest equanimity and a feeling that fate could not harm me now. Erchie was waiting to shepherd me, and asked me many curious questions about my visit. Strangely enough he did not appear to be inquisitive, nor did I feel inclined to resent his curiosity, but I was not in the least surprised to learn, many years afterwards, that the old man was one of Ian Maclaren's characters. There was undoubtedly much good " copy " in him.

Now although I never again made so long a journey for one lecture, and the expenses made a parlous hole in the fee, I could not help feeling that I was fairly launched, and that since my lecture had been well received by the assembled masters and uproariously hailed by the boys, I need no longer have any misgivings as to its reception anywhere. One resolution I then made which I have rigidly adhered to, and I am glad to know that through it many hundreds of schoolboys have blessed me. It was to avoid all appearance even of the pedagogue, of *swot* under the cloak of entertainment. I felt that since the boys had to come and had to pay to come, out of school hours too, the least I could do was to try and make my story as full of interest and fun as in me lay, and nothing has given me greater pleasure than to hear from old Public School boys all over the world when I have met them that I have succeeded.

When I reached home again I was much cheered to learn that the agency had secured me two engagements on consecutive days, one at Newcastle and the other at South Shields. This could only be looked upon by me as an opening into the larger lecture field, and I, who have always been the most diffident and self-distrustful of men, could not help feeling that I should be able to do full justice to my selection. My long experience in open-air preaching came to my recollection, those Sunday evenings on Peckham Rye, when thousands hung upon my words and I never had an angry voice raised against me, and I felt confident that as I knew all there was to be known about my subject, I could make it attractive to my audience. So that I never had the slightest mental trouble or foreboding about the result of these public lectures, while the fees marked against them struck me as being lavish gifts for what was going to be a most delightful holiday.

It must be remembered that up till this time I had belonged to that large stratum of society to whom the expenditure of a shilling for anything but the sternest necessaries of life is unthinkable—I gave up as hopeless the attempt to understand, for instance, how people could carelessly pay railway fares of pounds each when I could not have spared pennies for trams, often walking miles instead. As to those plutocrats who bought bicycles, watches, or hired cabs —well I realised that they moved in sublime regions far beyond my possible ken and dismissed them from my mind. But lecturing pushed me, without giving me time to think, into nearly all these things. I found myself buying a dress-suit, garments I had always associated with the idle rich, or waiters whom I had seen through the open doors of restaurants. I paid huge railway fares of nearly two sovereigns shudderingly, as if I were committing a crime, yet somehow remembering that these were part of the expenses which would be returnable. In fact, the whole of my outlook upon life was being changed.

Especially so in regard to what I may call the main-stay of my employment, the office. No one can ever know but myself how I loathed the place, how deeply sincere were the prayers I put up for deliverance from it. Yet I never could hope, for well I knew that the pay, though it remained at the same old two guineas a week for seventeen years and would, I knew, never be increased, was better than I could expect anywhere else as a clerk, and did I lose it, what prospect had I at between forty and fifty years of age of getting anything else? It is very likely that I was not worth more, indeed I dare say I was not, but then I knew the same of many others. That was not the trouble. It was the abominable system of petty persecution practised, the miserable tyranny exercised by those who were no higher in the social scale, had no reason to be ugly, except that they did no office work themselves and had perforce to make their juniors fill up the gap.

This it was that made me, when the first gleam of light came through the pall of cloud above me with the acceptance of the *Cruise of the Cachalot,* vow that at the very first opportunity given me I would take my courage in both hands and resign that magnificent appointment. Now all unknown to me that triumphant hour drew near. As usual several things combined to bring it about, but I believe the preeminent cause was this. My chief, before we were thus associated, had told me that he did not consider the writing of a private letter in office hours a wrong done to our employer the State. He might have added on his own behalf that the transaction of private business involving hours was venial, but he did not go as far as that. It happened, however, that one day when my correspondence was becoming heavier and more urgent than I could deal with at home that I *was* writing a private letter in office hours. My chief sternly invited me to put that private " work " away, refusing to look at it and see that it was a letter. I tried to explain and quoted his previous utterance on the subject. No use. He refused to discuss the matter, so I put the letter away and finished it in my luncheon three-quarters of an hour. It happened that it was an answer to a letter from the editor of a London newspaper offering me a salary exactly equivalent to my office pay for certain regular contributions. I made it an acceptance, and the next day I resigned.

Then I committed an unpardonable offence. For

firstly, I had taken nobody into my confidence; and, secondly, I had dared to do that which others with treble my earnings had longed to do but dared not. And to-day I am in certain quarters more bitterly hated than any man alive for this wickedness. However it did not matter to me, what did matter was my freedom and such a difference in treatment as I could not have believed possible. In fact I always feel a certain pride in the fact that I did manage to suppress the sense of being, and the appearance of having been, a drudge afraid to call my soul my own for all those years, and that I took my place in Society as naturally as if I had been born thereto.

Yes, amidst all that has befallen me since and in my present worn-out condition I can still feel grateful for the spirit that prompted me to shake the dust of that place off my feet and to tell those who had combined to make my life a burden to me while there, as they now fawned upon me, that for decency's sake they had better have kept silence, since nothing that they could say would ever efface the bitter impression of their utterly uncalled-for tyranny. Had I then known it, Nemesis was lying in wait for them, but I cared nothing for their future, having won clear of them and all their works I was content to ignore and as far as possible to forget them.

CHAPTER V

THE REAL BEGINNING

CHAPTER V

THE REAL BEGINNING

AND now behold me at the age of forty-two on the threshold of a new life. Already I could count four separate stages of an objectless career hopelessly leading nowhere, for even my sea-life, though I did manage to pass for chief mate at twenty-two, offered me no prospects save that of a drudge, a servant of servants at wretchedly inadequate pay. For it was a very dark hour for ships' officers. We walked the docks and thronged the shipping offices looking for berths and as often as not were driven to sea before the mast because we could not get berths as officers. And when we did the pay was such as seems incredible to-day. I have been offered (this was in 1881) £5 per month as chief mate of a 3000-ton tramp bound to the Baltic, and would have gladly accepted it but that a gentleman by the name of Gustave Shlum forestalled me. Eventually I did get a berth as chief officer of a brig sailing for the east coast of Africa at £5 15s. per month, but then I had to sign an agreement to be responsible for all cargo short delivered. And I worked harder than anybody

else on board except the splendid bos'un—carpenter—
second mate, who was a Russian Finn and was priceless
—I have never seen so good a man except once and
he was filling a similar position and hailed from the
same place, Helsingfors.

Still, as a dear friend, Sir Arthur Conan Doyle,
once told me, it was all experience, and now I was to
enjoy the ripened fruit of it, although the marvel
was that these soul-withering years that the locust
had eaten had not destroyed all memory of those
exciting days. It had not in the least, and I looked
forward calmly and confidently, without the least
doubt of my ability to " make good," even though
I was beginning at the very beginning and that too
at a time of life when most men are fixed for life.
My new appointment was on the staff of the *Morning
Leader*, and my duty was to write three one-column
articles a week on nautical topics, my salary being
£104 per annum. True I had an empty home and a
wife and four children dependent upon me, but I
was used to the burden, and, moreover, I could earn
my salary by about two hours' work three times a
week, never having the slightest difficulty in finding
topics, and able to work anywhere.

But best of all, I could fulfil lecture engagements
without asking leave of anybody, which I felt might
be a great boon in the near future when such engagements began to pour in. And another thing, I found
work at very remunerative rates flowing in upon me,

so that I was soon able to ask and receive better prices. Also, accumulating a little store of money I was able to repay debts that my creditors had long before wiped off their books as hopeless. So that, taking it by and large, as we used to say, I commenced my lecturing career under the fairest auspices and set off for the north to fulfil my first two engagements under the Lecture Agency without any but the most pleasurable anticipations.

A couple of days before starting I received a very stiff and formal invitation to accept the hospitality of a member of the Society for which I was to lecture. It was simply signed " Wm. Lowrie," and gave me not the slightest intimation as to who the writer might be. But I was in a most responsive mood, open to every kindly influence, and I wrote accepting gratefully. And it was with a sense of real grateful surprise that I found my host, a grave dignified man about twenty years my senior, with shipmaster writ large all over him, awaiting my arrival with a carriage. How we knew each other I cannot tell, that has always been one of the mysteries to me, the numbers of times I have been met by entire strangers who have picked me out from among a crowd of passengers—but I know that in five minutes we were close friends.

I found to my amazement that I was the guest of one of the classic figures of the old sailing-ship days. A man who had served his time in the Arctic whalers out of Peterhead, had been officer in such historic clippers as the *Marco Polo*, the *Schomberg*, *James Baines* and *Redjacket* and also in the ship about which Dickens turned the vials of his just wrath on the War Office authorities of the day for the callous way in which they destroyed the lives of time-expired soldiers from India on the passage home and on landing. She will remain evermore infamous in history as the *Great Tasmania*, though Dickens expressly exempts from his censure her crew.

Only an old sailor could understand my delight at meeting such a man, who was withal so modest and kind. The only drawback I felt was in what I considered the over-emphasis of his praise for what I had written about the sea. But then seamen are all prone to overrate the value of matter written about the life they know by men who have lived that life. Their appreciation is in just proportion to their scorn of the many modern writers who on the strength of a broken apprenticeship or a homeward passage round Cape Horn thenceforth pose as nautical experts and complacently allow themselves to be called Captain This or That when they do not know enough seamanship to cross a royal yard.

I spent a most enjoyable three days in Newcastle for the lectures were a great success, and my life in my host's delightful company full of such a pleasure as I have never experienced before. For in addition to his great eminence in the world I knew so well, he was kindness and considerateness itself and never once forgot to make my welfare his first thought. I regret to cease talking about him, but must remember the claims of others, so I will only add here that our friendship lasted as long as he lived, about ten years. He left between £30,000 and £40,000, practically the whole of which has gone to the benefit of seamen.

Now I have no knowledge of the means used by the Lecture Agency to spread the fame of a lecturer and get him engagements, I only know that after my performances at Newcastle and Shields engagements began to pour in, some to my amazement and secret pride from the great classic Public Schools. These engagements did not come singly either. For instance, I received in one bunch bookings for eight different institutes around Birmingham, all of which were within a short distance, under half an hour's journey from the centre of the City. I afterwards learned that it was the highly commendable practice of the secretaries of these institutes to meet and arrange their lecture dates so that a lecturer could go from one to the other on successive nights, thus giving him the minimum of travel and expense and enabling him to take lower fees with no monetary disadvantage to himself. Unhappily that good practice has come to an end for nearly all the institutes are no more, at least so I was told by the secretary of one who claimed to be the last survivor.

Speaking of Birmingham, an experience befell me

there which is one of the most salient memories of that interesting time. It also shows how little I yet knew of what I may call the intricacies of railway travel in my own country. I was booked to lecture at the Birmingham Town Hall (I had never yet been to the City) at 7 p.m. one Sunday, and chose the L. and N.W. I did not trouble to look at the G.W. time-tables or I might have found, as I did recently, an incomparably better and quicker train with a luncheon car attached. However, I joined the train at Willesden at about 10 a.m. and giving a porter my bag asked him to put me in the Birmingham portion of the train, although I did not then know that any part of the train went anywhere else.

I found a comfortable seat, and when the train stopped at Rugby I went to the refreshment room and bought a penny loaf, bread having been omitted from the nose-bag I carried as suspecting no food arrangements. I rejoined the train, lunched comfortably, and went to sleep afterwards, waking up to find the train passing through Rugeley. Now my scanty geographical knowledge of England told me that something was wrong, an idea which was confirmed when the train drew up at Stafford. Alighting in great trepidation, I sought an official who told me that the next train back to Birmingham was due to arrive there at 8 p.m.—it was then 2 p.m.—but he added abstractedly, "It generally don't get there much afore half-past." And my lecture was at 7!

I am fairly well able to keep my head under any circumstances, but I confess that I was really daunted now. Thirty miles from Birmingham on a Sunday afternoon. I thought of a bike, madness! Taxis had not been thought of yet, and a special train was out of the question. So I sat down and allowed my mind to rest awhile—that is I didn't think of anything for a few minutes. But a genial porter came along who must have seen a certain woe-begone look in my face, for he accosted me with a cheery "What's up, governor?"

I immediately poured my sad story into his ears as plainly as possible. When I had finished he smiled brightly and said:

"You see our stationmaster, governor; he'll put you right, you see if he don't. Fine old cock our stationmaster is."

I confess that I did not feel hopeful, but the man's manner was infectious and, moreover, I was ready, like a drowning man, to catch at any straw. So I begged him to lead me to the stationmaster. That worthy was one of the jolliest-looking old men I have ever seen, and his very appearance was comforting. He heard me tell my tale, then said cheerfully:

"You're all right, young man; Sunday is the very best day for getting anywhere, although the time-table knows nothing about that. I've got no less than four theatrical specials coming through this afternoon, any one of which would drop you at

F

Brum. I'll stop the first one for you and you'll get to New Street about 3.30. How will that suit you?"

Well, I'll leave it to you. I am glad to say that I tipped that good porter a florin in my gratitude, and according to promise found myself going up Corporation Street at half-past three. But when at about 6.40 I made my way to Chamberlain Square and saw it black with people all making their way to the magnificent classical building in the centre, I fell a-trembling to think that I might have disappointed that vast crowd. In fact I had hardly recovered myself when the time came for me to go on the platform. But the sight I then saw steadied me. The vast building was crowded to its utmost capacity and I looked upon a veritable sea of heads. The platform and orchestra were also crowded, only leaving a small oblong for me.

After the singing of a hymn and the reading of some notices I was introduced and the volume of cheering that greeted me brought a big lump into my throat, for I was totally unprepared for it as well as unused to such a greeting. My subject was " Romance and Reality at Sea," and I can say without boasting that not even the great Birmingham orator could have held that audience better. I had been told to cease at the hour, and obedient to instructions I did so, telling the audience why. A mighty shout went up of " Go on, go on," so I went on for another half-hour, receiving such an ovation as I closed that I was fairly stupefied. Many hundreds of lectures have I enjoyed since then and have received as much appreciation as any man ought to have, but that night in Brum overtops them all. And I was within an ace of missing it altogether!

While I am on this topic I will say that in the fairly long time, about fifteen years, that I have been lecturing I cannot say that I have ever lost an appointment by the fault of the railway. I have been late certainly, but on the one occasion when I missed my engagement altogether it was entirely my own fault. No, many are the grievances that lecturers have, and hold legitimately, against the railway companies, but losing engagements by reason of railway unpunctuality is not one of them. I may as well say here that it always has seemed to me little short of an outrage that lecturers, who yearly spend enormous sums in railway travelling, should have no concession whatever made to them, while golfers and commercial travellers are allowed to travel at such greatly reduced rates. Perhaps the most galling thing of all is to take a ticket on Saturday for some distant place for which the ordinary fare is high and because you must return the same night be compelled to pay the full ordinary fare, while an ordinary week-end ticket will be less than half the money. Or to book at the same time as a golfer, pay nearly double the fare he does and go and return in the same compartment. Not only so, but the train will stop at an unscheduled station for him while the lecturer may plead for the same privilege in vain.

In order to have my growl upon a particular instance, I should like to state that once having a lecture at New Barnet and the time of its close not allowing me to catch the 9.50 at Finsbury Park, I, holding a first-class season ticket between London and Melbourn, Cambs, where I lived, applied to the High Gods at King's Cross for permission to have that particular train stopped at New Barnet to allow me to get home that night. I felt the more emboldened to ask this concession because express trains were being continually stopped at Knebworth for golfers and at Foxton for one gentleman who lived near the station. My application was curtly refused without reason assigned. Yet only three days afterwards I received from King's Cross a touting letter stating that as they had noticed that I was billed to lecture in Sheffield on a certain date, they begged to call my attention to the advantages of travelling by their line and would gladly book me a third- or first-class seat, whichever I preferred.

I hope I did justice to the matter in my reply to that letter, but as I had no reply from them I am not sure. One more anecdote of a similar nature and I leave the subject for the time. I once booked on a Monday two first-class return tickets to the Hague and round Belgium and Holland for the following Saturday. Ultra-honest, I enclosed a cheque for the full amount post-dated for Friday. I received the usual post-card acknowledgment and dismissed the matter from my mind. On arriving at Liverpool Street, fifteen minutes before the departure of the train at 8 p.m., and applying for my tickets I was told that they could not be issued without present payment and that my post-dated cheque had been returned. It had not, and I have never since seen it, but the salient fact was that I had not sufficient cash with me to meet this large item and I had to give up my journey.

Since then I have never sent any money upon booking seats in a train and I rejoice to say that the mutual confidence has never been abused, the results have always been entirely satisfactory, which is in startling contrast to continental practice, where no seat will be booked for you unless you pay your fare at the time. But a truce to railway matters for a time, although as they form so large a portion of a lecturer's experiences I make no apology for alluding to them at such length.

CHAPTER VI

SCOTLAND

CHAPTER VI

SCOTLAND

MY second season was a very full one, but what I think gave me more pleasure than anything connected with it was the fact that I had about three weeks in Scotland. For I had only made one flying visit to Scotland before except as a sailor and then very briefly, seeing only the seamy sides of Glasgow and Dundee. But I had delightful remembrances of Scotsmen the world over, and especially in New Zealand; some of my most dearly loved shipmates had been Scotsmen and I flattered myself that I could pass as a Scotsman anywhere in any northern dialect except that of Glasgow, which I confess always bothered me.

Now, not having had the advantage of conferring with any of my fellow-lecturers I was just a little anxious to know whether my countrymen's notion had any ground for it, viz. that a Scotsman, or an assembly of them, could not see a joke and were very chary of showing any sign of appreciation. I had a fairly wide range for testing, for my engagements ranged from Dumfries to Oban, Perth to Hawick.

I do not now remember which town or city I began in, but I think it was Oban. My host was a local school-master, of quite straitened means I should judge, but a kindly gentleman if ever there was one. The lecture hall was a drill shed and a very rough one at that, but it seemed exactly suited to my audience, who struck me as being one and all working folk. But the gravity of their demeanour, the intelligence they displayed in taking up every point, and the whole-hearted enjoyment with which they greeted even my feeblest jokes made me love them. Indeed I was so carried away by their interest that I committed that well-nigh unpardonable crime in a lecturer—I went on for two hours instead of ending at one hour and a half, beyond which time it is wicked to expect any person to be attentive.

When at last the lecture was over I was met in the stable-like ante-room by a grave committee of poorly dressed men who quietly thanked me for the pleasure I had given them, and one (who really looked as if he did not earn so much in six months) pro-duced a dingy bag and counted out my heavy fee in gold upon the rough table, producing at the same time a form of receipt. It was the first time I had ever been paid for a lecture like that, and it made me feel rather strange, the amount seemed so large compared with the surroundings and its source. But I consoled myself with the thought that the committee did not appear the sort of men who would purchase an article unless they knew they were getting their money's worth.

My next engagement was at Dundee, and as it was midwinter I was confronted with a rough journey across Scotland of great length in point of time. But I consoled myself with the knowledge that there was to be a long wait at Dunblane, where I could rest in a warm room and have a good hot meal, for the excellence of Scotch hotels had long been known to me by repute. Also, but I do not know why, "Jessie, the flower o' Dunblane," kept running through my mind, making the prospect of visiting the place quite alluring.

The train arrived there in a blizzard of snow, and I lost no time in transferring myself, making sure of the time of departure of my Dundee train and securing information from the porter as to the whereabouts of the principal hotel. I was chilled to the marrow when I got there, for Dunblane seemed dead beyond resurrection and buried under snow. And when I entered the hotel I saw no one, but following painted instructions went upstairs, where I found a splendid room with a long table laid for a banquet. I rang the bell and seated myself, rejoicing in the thought of what was to come.

Alas, a veritable draggle-tailed Sally Slap-cabbage answered my call, and her first words to me were:

"Ye maun c'way oot o' that, it's privaat."

Law-abiding ever, I rose with alacrity, only asking

where I could go to be comfortable. She showed me into a dark, fireless, dirty cell, and said nonchalantly:

"D'ye wish tea?"

I replied briskly, "No, I want dinner, and as quick as possible. Also a fire or another room, this is as cold as the open air."

"We've nae denner," was the reply, "an' I dinna ken if ther any cauld meat, but ye can hae some tea, an' I'll see if ther's ony meat."

She departed and after twenty minutes' absence returned with a dish whereon were a few dirty scraps of cold mutton, obviously scraped from the bone. Some tea and bread and butter of a parsimonious and poverty-stricken sort completed the banquet, which, however it disgusted me, was so certainly all there was obtainable that I made no further protest but ate and shivered in silence. When I came to pay I was charged two shillings, which the taciturn Moll accepted in silence and I departed colder than when I arrived and extremely anxious never to renew my acquaintance with Dunblane any more.

But all my discontent vanished upon arrival at Dundee. Though it was snowing heavily my kind and thoughtful host, Bailie Robertson, was at the station to meet me and I very soon found myself in his beautiful house seated before a noble hot meal which was ready and waiting for me, and at which that splendid old lady his sister presided with a motherly grace that I can never forget. As both these grand old people are dead I can speak of them with greater freedom than they would have liked during their lifetime, for they were essentially of the kind who " do good by stealth, and blush to find it fame."

Here again my lecture effort gave me the greatest possible gratification. Not only was the fine Kinnaird Hall packed with listeners, but a large portion of them were intimately connected with the whale fishery and were therefore intensely interested in my subject, although I spoke mainly upon the Southern Whale Fishery, a totally different business. I cannot remember how many old whaling skippers were introduced to me after the lecture, but I do remember and shall always be grateful for their very warm appreciation and the outspoken manner in which they gave it utterance. But I hope and believe that I realised then, and always have done, that their tribute was paid, not to any eloquence or oratory, but to practical acquaintance with the great business with which I dealt, and that I think will always be found to be the case with every subject. That it should be so seems eminently reasonable.

Now lest it should appear that my lecture path was roses, roses all the way, I must just interpose an experience in Scotland of a very different character. I was booked to lecture at Borrowstounness (Bo'ness) at a very low fee because it " fitted in " as we say; that is because I had other lectures in Scotland round about that time, obviating the necessity for making a long journey from London specially. Now I had to come from Hull, leaving there at 6 a.m., and in consequence when I arrived in Edinburgh, where I had to spend three or four hours, I was very tired. Common prudence would suggest that I should have a quiet meal and a rest, but I was not prudent, and, having ascertained the time of a convenient train from Waverley to Bo'ness, I used up my spare time in visiting friends in Edinburgh.

Therefore when I joined my train I settled down and went fast asleep, so fast, that I did not awake to change at Manuel Junction. I did awake at Falkirk, the next station, and there found that the next train back to Bo'ness would not get me there much before nine o'clock, my lecture being fixed for eight. Knowing that Falkirk was not far from Bo'ness by road, I then begged the stationmaster to tell me where I could get a " masheen," as a wheeled vehicle is called up here, to take me the nine miles, and how much the charge was likely to be. For all reply he waved his hand in a lordly manner towards a row of cabs ranged outside the station, and I, as it was then 6.30 o'clock and I felt that I had no time to lose, immediately interviewed a cabman. But no inducement that I could offer up to £2 had any effect upon the frozen stolidity of those men, I could get nothing out of them but a surly " No."

So at last I had to wire to the secretary, informing

him of the state of affairs, and saying that I could not hope to reach him before nine o'clock. Of course I got no answer and when I arrived the little platform was crowded with what would have been my audience, reinforced by all the loafers and bad boys in the town. For the only time in my life I was booed and hissed, but I feel grateful that nobody threw anything or I should certainly have been pelted also. This, though unpleasant, did not hurt me so much as the attitude of the secretary. He did not actually call me a liar, but he said that though several lecturers, notably Mary Kingsley, had missed that Manuel connection before, none had ever experienced any difficulty in getting a masheen to bring them from Falkirk. Drivers were always eager to take the job, besides, there was a posting-house opposite the station, and the fare was 10s. In vain I told him my experience, his only reply was, " It's verra strange." And his look said quite plainly, " You are telling me lies." In the end I was compelled to make a journey from London some months later to give that lecture, the expenses of which left me with a slight balance on the wrong side when I had received my fee.

As a set off to this decidedly unpleasant experience I shortly afterwards paid a visit to Penicuik, and became the guest of Mr. S. R. Crockett. The whole of that visit is like a blissful dream, for verily I never enjoyed myself more. The big genial novelist, then in the heyday of his prosperity, was an ideal host and even outdid his countrymen in his efforts to make his guest happy. But of all the delights of that happy three days one experience stands out, salient, from the rest. It was Mr. Crockett's prayer at family worship on the night of my arrival. As a general rule I dread to hear extempore prayer, having often suffered many things from men who either maundered or preached or raved and foamed and pounded for long periods of time and assumed that they were *praying!* But that prayer was in my mind all that a prayer ought to be and as a proof of this it is the only one, out of the many thousands I have heard and mostly writhed under, that I joyfully and gratefully remember. Only a few days ago I heard that my good friend and host of that occasion had passed away from us in the fullness of his powers and manhood. And though I only forgathered with him once I have an aching sense of irreplaceable loss.

Following hard upon the heels of that came another delightful experience, a lecture at Fettes College, when I had the privilege of making the acquaintance of Dr. Heard, the headmaster, whose guest I was. That acquaintance deepened into friendship, second of the many headmasters whom it has been my fortunate lot to know and love and about whom I hope to fill many pages. But on the very threshold of the subject I must pause to note my astonishment, not that some headmasters relegate the duty of showing hospitality to some person other than themselves, but that any headmaster dares to invite such strangers as lecturers and entertainers must be, to stay with him at all.

For I have heard such stories, not told in malice, but sadly, and with an obvious effort to gloss over the worst features, as have made me redden with shame, stories that have fully explained to me the aloofness with which I have sometimes been regarded where I was not known. Stories of hospitality abused, of persistent and vehement begging, of equally persistent touting for employment, backed by assurances that without that particular engagement the wheels would come right off the applicant's carriage—how can men, expecting to be received and treated as gentlemen, and never expecting in vain, be guilty of such behaviour? But then I have known tradesmen who, upon receiving an order upon the fulfilment of which they have been promptly paid, immediately proffer a request for a substantial loan. This, I suppose, would be on the ground that a man who would pay lawful demands like that *must* have more money than he knew what to do with, and must also be somewhat easy in his hold upon that money.

Now the gentry whom I have hinted at as abusing the confidence of headmaster hosts would undoubtedly be indignant at being classed with tradesmen, but if there be any truth in the grand old adage, *noblesse oblige*, they are far more culpable. But I hold that

G

the average tradesman's standard is higher than theirs and with less reason.

My visit to Fettes, following as it did upon the beautiful experience of Penicuik, went far to confirm me in my opinion that the lecturer's life was a charming one, the people were all so pleasant, so eager to make one happy and comfortable. Moreover, it was a delight to address the lads. Of course it was impossible to tell how they would have received the lecture had they been perfectly free agents, but that is one of those things about which it is well never to show too much curiosity. All one could do, and that was certainly obligatory in the highest sense, was to give them one's best and make it as interesting as possible; as I have before hinted, that is, to allow no suspicion of " swot " to creep in under the disguise of an entertainment.

But undoubtedly it is a little difficult sometimes to hold the attention of the very youngest boys, whose minds are often incapable of sustained effort. Occasionally this is manifested to the lecturer in a startling manner, as the following experience of mine at a preparatory school at West Drayton will show. I was speaking upon " Romance and Reality at Sea," amid an ominous quiet on the part of my very juvenile audience which gave me the uneasy consciousness that I was often outside their depth. A lecturer can always tell whether his audience be with him or not, whatever be their ages or conditions. Suddenly there broke from the boys a spontaneous peal of laughter, so ringing, so universal that I almost fancied hysteria had seized upon them, and wondered whether I was to blame. I could not imagine anything I had said causing such an outburst. I stood facing the roaring lads waiting for the merriment to subside and puzzled beyond belief, until I suddenly turned and looked at the screen and the mystery was at once cleared up.

A full-rigged sailing ship was being shown, and walking across her maintopmast stay was a fly magnified to the size of an eagle. It had evidently got into the condenser somehow, and finding it warm moved about pretty briskly, but, of course, never out of the picture. It had obviously come as a sweet boon, a heavenly relief from boredom, and the children had welcomed it thus uproariously in consequence. And I regret to say that neither my eloquence nor the commands of the masters availed to restore the youngsters' attention. So we presently gave it up as a bad job, at which announcement the laughter burst forth again as if irrepressible.

I leave any moral that may be drawn from this episode to those whose interest it is to seek it, I have no concern with the matter now beyond relating facts and uttering the platitude that it is unwise to expect too much from young boys.

CHAPTER VII

JOURNEYS

CHAPTER VII

JOURNEYS

THERE is one thing about a lecturer's experiences which has always been a mystery to me, though it has not been so much so since the advent of the picture palace. It is that one continually finds oneself going to places whose very names have hitherto been hidden from a fairly intelligent, well-travelled man, while great towns with many thousands of inhabitants seem to pass you by in silent disdain. I will not quote the names of those big towns lest I should find that there is a reason uncomplimentary to myself in their neglect of my services, but the fact is as I have stated and is in no wise peculiar to my own experience.

But some of those out-of-the-way places; what a wealth of memories they do recall; nearly all, I am happy to say, of a genial pleasant character, albeit the journey to some of them was a pilgrimage of pain. Indeed I have often wondered how it was that I, one of the frailest of men, with especially weak bronchial apparatus, have never " cracked up " on those wretched journeys. Recollections of them come crowding thick and fast, but I think I must award the palm of discomfort to one that was only difficult to reach by reason of a mistake, not on my part. I was due to lecture at Masham in Yorkshire on a certain evening on the morning of which I was at Huddersfield.

Trusting to information given me by a railway official at Huddersfield instead of to the local time-table (a mistake of mine), I arrived at Leeds to find that I could not make my connection through Ripon to Masham in time. So I wired to the stationmaster at Ripon asking him if he would kindly secure me a conveyance to Masham, distant ten miles. I duly arrived at Ripon to find awaiting me a dog-cart with a huge Yorkshire horse between the shafts and a typical Tyke holding the reins. There was also, the time being December, a bitter blasting north-east gale blowing over the moors, and of course I had left my heavy fur-lined overcoat at Huddersfield. I may say in passing that I dreaded to wear it for many reasons, but chiefly because of the chivying of the small boy.

We started, and before we had gone a mile I was congealed. Cold! Well, I don't know exactly, but I was past feeling and only conscious of a dull desire that the truly infernal wind would cease blowing for just five minutes. But it never did, and at the end of one of the longest hours I have ever known, much longer than a trick at the wheel off the Horn, and God knows they were long enough (but I was young then), we surged into Masham, arriving at the hall an hour before the lecture was due. I was directed to the most hospitable abode of the local bank manager, who had invited me to stay with him (only I had never received the letter), and given such restoratives as kindness dictated.

He pressed me to stay the night, but I had booked my room at the hotel in Ripon and the trap had to go back, so I, newly warmed and fed, refused. The lecture went off with a bang as usual, and amid a chorus of congratulations and commiseration I mounted the trap again—and so home to the hotel, through a stronger wind and a light snowfall. Arriving at the hotel I had to be lifted out of the trap and carried into the bar parlour, where I was thawed out, while my driver, the burly taciturn giant, drank cold ale and looked pityingly, albeit with wonder, upon the weakling he had brought back.

A bonny fire was kindled in my room and boots and ostler carried me upstairs. Native delicacy, I suppose, prevented them valeting me, so it was with many a groan and much effort I got out of my clothes and between the blankets. And my last thought was that I was booked for a long stay—as to going to Sedbergh on the following day the idea was too ridiculous to entertain. Yet on awaking in the morning I was up and partly dressed before I remembered my parlous condition of the previous night, and it is not one of the least strange things in my strange life that this has ever been the case. Going to bed utterly beaten and apparently in for a long illness and rising next morning able to resume the war-path. I suppose it must be a remanet from the days when I couldn't give in, like so many men and women in the same toilful walk of life.

Another journey of horror which comes into my mind at this time was one I made to the favourite watering-place of Lytham, but owing to the fact that I was also to speak on Sunday as well as lecture on Monday it was necessary that I should leave London on Saturday. Not being able to ascertain from the intricacies of Bradshaw anything definite as to the time of my arrival, I enquired at Euston and was informed that I could get a train at Preston for Lytham at about 4.30 a.m. (I speak loosely as to time, it being so long ago), arriving at Lytham somewhere about three hours later. Whereupon I booked and left Euston about ten o'clock, arriving at Preston somewhere about 2 a.m. I sought a first-class waiting-room, for in those palmy days I always travelled first class, but I found it full of a foul crowd of men, smoking, swearing, and spitting, and entirely resentful of my intrusion, especially so of my fur coat.

I quietly retired to the farthest corner of the room, wondering much but far too wise to say anything, and with my rug for a covering and my bag for a pillow laid me down upon one side of a big table that stood there. In spite of the devilish uproar I was soon asleep, but I was rudely awakened by being jerked off the table on to the befouled floor, amid a perfect tempest of delight. I picked myself up and silently collected my belongings amid the hoots and jeers of the crowd. And out upon that wind-swept platform I sought a resting-place on a bench (shelter from the wind there was none) and lay there wide awake until 4.30 a.m. I may here interpolate that letters addressed to Euston on the subject of this curious use of first-class waiting-rooms at Preston and Chester never even met with the courtesy of a reply.

Somewhere about 4.30 a train came in, and I, feeling a spasm of hope, made for it, finding a good fellow-porter who told me that it was going to Manchester and furthermore volunteered his opinion that no train for Lytham would go before ten o'clock.

" But," he said, " I'll make sure for ye, an' if I'm right you might go to the Park Hotel an' be comfortable." Judging by my fur coat he doubtless thought that the expense didn't matter. Of course he was right, and I made the pilgrimage along that lengthy bridge to the hotel, suitably rewarding (I hope) my friendly porter with a shilling. Then I said to the night porter of the hotel:

" Please do not call me on any account until 9.30, as my train does not go until 10.30, and I want to get warm. Bring me up a cup of tea and some bread and butter and my bill at 9.30 and all will be well."

He nodded and left me. I turned in, but sleep was out of the question. I heard five strike and six and seven and then, whatever was that diabolical knocking?

"What is it?" I roared. "Hot water," was the reply. Then I realised that I had been to sleep and I got out of bed, switched on the light, looked at my watch and behold it was 7.40. I am not a hot-tempered man and should have made an ineffectual despot, but if that night porter had been at my absolute disposal then—I really would not like to say. Of course I got no more sleep, and equally of course I had to pay full charge for bed and breakfast. And I have hated Preston Station with a perfect hatred ever since. I suppose all the fraternity are like that—have their special likes and dislikes among stations as amongst people.

Pocklington is a name branded upon my memory, not because of its school, of which I have heard many excellent reports, but know nothing, but because I have made two visits there to lecture and each time have been filled with wonder and laughter. The secretary and mainstay of the lecture society was (and is for all I know) a genial eccentric doctor, a widower living with his daughter. The lecture hall might be a stable or a barn or a shed of sorts, I only know that when I first entered it the audience was clustered round the stove in the centre and the whole scene was worthy of a picture by Rembrandt. I had a queer feeling that none of my audience had ever heard a lecture before, which was absurd, for I know that many of my colleagues had entertained them, but they looked at me as though they thought I might bite, and I looked at them cheerfully as I would have done at a mob of Australian blackfellows. Me !

Yet the lectures were a success. We had a good time together. By the way, I often wonder what a leviathan of Johnson's calibre would do with a crowd like that. He would probably antagonise the bulk of them before he had been speaking five minutes, because nothing annoys an audience like that more than what they call " putting the pot on," and I cannot help feeling much sympathy for them. In fact the more I read Boswell's Johnson the more murderously I feel towards him, and the more prone I am to regard him as the most wrongly puffed-up bully that ever lived. That, however, is a mere matter of opinion and Johnson would probably have disposed of it in one flatulent breath.

What, however, I could not get over in Pocklington was the hotel. It was one of the old-timers and all its staff were genuinely anxious to make the guest comfortable. But to go downstairs half dressed in the morning, find after long enquiry a key, and then traverse a long wet yard in search of relief, these were matters that left their indelible trace, in England, where a man over forty gets soft and slack and notices such things. Yet people go abroad and endure them and never murmur. How is it, I wonder? I read endless encomia upon foreign ways, foreign cooking, foreign politeness, but never a word about foreign dirt, foreign stenches, foreign absence of sanitary arrangements. What a mystery!

It will be a little relief to get my mind off this business of foreign hotels to recall an experience which if it did not amuse me at the time certainly did both interest and amuse my one fellow-passenger. I booked first class as I usually did in those days from Huddersfield to Manchester, where I was due to lecture at the Athenæum at eight, but where I had no offer of hospitality. The train by which I travelled was timed to arrive in Manchester at about seven, ample time for me to find a hotel, change, get a meal, and arrive at the Athenæum by 7.50. But by some accident or stupidity I got into the wrong part of the train and after a long wait at Stalybridge I became disagreeably aware that something was wrong. Indeed I was past the time I had reckoned on arriving at Manchester before we left Stalybridge, and the train was going very deliberately.

At last I saw plainly that if I was going to get to my lecture in time it was all I should do, and turning to my sole fellow-passenger with whom, after the custom of Englishmen, I had not as yet exchanged a word, I said:

" Excuse me, sir, but do you mind if I change my clothes? I am due to lecture at the Athenæum at eight and I fear that I have made a mistake in the train."

He replied instantly: "Go ahead, for this train isn't due in until 7.55. Don't mind me."

I thanked him and began, but oh, just then the train began to cut capers and my corresponding movements about that compartment must have been amazing. My fellow-passenger laughed himself ill, especially when, struggling into a " biled " shirt I was hurled, with both my arms prisoned, from one side of the compartment to the other. Indeed his merriment had little cessation, for similar evolutions took place as I got into my trousers, fastened my collar, and made my white bow. When at last I had finished and he lay utterly exhausted on the cushions, he gasped out :

" Well, sir, I've never laughed so much in all my life and I'll come to hear you lecture, for I feel anxious to know how such a preparation will affect you. Besides, I need a sedative and I guess a lecture is the sort of thing to quiet the most edgy nerves."

I nodded, smiling grimly at his awkward compliment, so typical of the north, and just then the train rolled into the station on time. Giving my bag to a porter and telling him to get me a cab, I bolted to the refreshment room where I got a glass of port and snatched a couple of hard-boiled eggs. The hall couldn't have been many yards from the station for half the second egg was in my fingers and the other half in my mouth when we arrived there. And I am afraid I was still swallowing when I stood up and faced the audience.

Of course the lecture went off all right, they always did somehow, but my greatest triumph that night was being met by my railway acquaintance, who lugged me off to his favourite hotel and insisted upon footing my bill, because, he said, I'd given him the jolliest half-day's entertainment he'd ever had in his days, and one that would serve him with experiences to tell at his club, etc., for the rest of his life.

Another experience of a similar kind occurs to me, but the preliminaries were even more painful or wearing than this last. I was booked to lecture at Willenhall, a suburb of Wolverhampton, and came from London to keep my appointment. But my train broke down at Roade and by the time we got to New Street the connection for Willenhall had vanished, of course. However, the courteous station-master arranged for the train to be stopped at Willen-hall to allow me to alight. So it was, but a howling mob of colliers filled the platform and though my bag got out I couldn't. ·Vainly did the guard shout " keep back," the crowd pressed in and the train moved off. I sprang out at the first opportunity, alighting on my back and rolling over several times, feeling very foolish when at last I remembered where I was, without the remarks of the stationmaster and porters, which tended to rub that fact in.

When I was able to move off I did so without comment, for I felt that any attempt of mine to reply would be entirely unworthy of the occasion. Outside the station I was assailed by a mob of ragged urchins competing for the job of carrying my bag, and selecting one, who was escorted by the rest, I arrived at the hall in about five minutes. I was met by the tired-looking secretary, to whom I commenced to apologise for its being ten minutes past eight, but he cut me short by saying :

"Don't worry, the lanternist isn't here yet!" Whereupon I suggested that I would change into platform rig if a corner could be found for me, and I was duly shown by the caretaker into his kitchen—living-room. Whew! I then realised that I was in the land of cheap coal, for I should think there must have been a couple of hundredweights on the fire. The room was so hot that by the time I had finished dressing the beautiful front of my dress shirt was limp as a piece of blotting-paper and I was nearly suffocated.

And still poor Perry hadn't turned up. If ever he sees these words he'll remember that awful night. I don't know what the time was when he arrived, but I know that when at last he was ready for me it was past nine and the audience had been sitting patiently waiting—most of them—since 7.30. I went on and apologised for Perry and myself, putting all the blame where it belonged, on the railway company,

H

for Perry's failure was due to his lantern and cylinders of gas having been put off at some junction, Handsworth, I think, while he went on sublimely unconscious to Willenhall. And it was all the more reprehensible because, as he said, he was as well known on the lines all around Brum as one of the railway officials themselves. I didn't suffer much, but it was a terrible experience for him, he being a man of considerable weight and the night stuffy.

A curious reminiscence of mine is concerning a lecture I gave at Hebden Bridge, one of those quaint, most picturesque manufacturing villages in the northern part of the West Riding of Yorkshire. I was not offered hospitality nor had I any previous correspondence with the secretary of the society engaging me, but that was nothing out of the common and after enquiry I made for the only hotel in the place (as far as I know). I was feeling very fit and comfortable after dinner as I sat smoking and awaiting eight o'clock, the hall being just across the road.

Suddenly, to me entered two men, with gloomy looks and an air of embarrassment, who seeing me in evening dress at once concluded that I was the lecturer and introduced themselves as secretary and treasurer respectively of the society engaging me. Then the secretary stammered out:

" We've come on rather a curious errand, Mr. Bullen. We've come to ask you if you'll take your fee and go away ? "

"Of course, if you wish it," I replied, with a smile of encouragement; "but surely you don't mind telling me why, though perhaps I ought not to enquire." (The treasurer had meanwhile stealthily placed a little pile of gold at my elbow.)

"Well, you see, it's like this," grunted the secretary, with a brick-red flush on his face, "there's nobody there. An' there's nobody to come, as far as I can see. The men folk are almost all gone and th' women don't care. So the society's cracked up. Anyhow, I'm done with it from to-night; I don't like this kind of job at all. However, we're much obliged t'ye, Mr. Bullen."

"Oh, not at all," I chortled gaily, as I absent-mindedly slipped the sovereigns into my breeches pocket. "But if anybody *should* come between now and half-past nine I'm quite willing to give the lecture, even if there's only half a dozen present."

With more muttered thanks they left me, and I sat smiling at my own thoughts, gazing at the fire and feeling very comfortable. At about half-past eight, however, the secretary peeped in again and said very apologetically:

"There's a few people come, sir, so we thought perhaps you wouldn't mind——"

"Why, of course," I cried gaily, and springing up I accompanied him to the platform of the really fine hall (seating capacity about four hundred, I should think) and gave my lecture to less than a dozen people.

What did it matter when the lights were turned down ?
And so we parted on the best of terms with each other,
and I to bed feeling very virtuous.

Now this was Saturday night and I was due to
lecture at Halifax on the morrow at seven p.m. So
I planned to have a comfortable midday meal where
I was and get on by a good train in the afternoon.
But after breakfast the waitress, a typical Yorkshire
lass, enquired, but without a trace of interest :

" When are ye goin' ? "

I informed her courteously of my intentions and
she replied, again with that air of aloofness :

" Ye'll have to go afore dinner."

" But why ? " I remonstrated. " I'm very comfortable here. And I don't want to go before
dinner."

" There's no dinner served in this house on Sunday,"
she responded indifferently.

I looked at her abstractedly for a few moments as
she finished clearing the table, and then as she was
leaving the room I asked her if she'd be kind enough
to ask the landlord or landlady to come and see me.
She did not answer, but in about a minute a stout,
comely dame appeared with the light of battle in
her eye. To her I addressed myself, treating the
waitress's communication as sheer irresponsible froth.
But I was suddenly cut short by the dame, who ex-
ploded :

" Thirty-five year I've kept this house and I've

never served owt in it of a Sunday except breakfast, an' I never will."

I began to feel a little warm myself now, and quietly suggested that by the Innkeepers' Act she was bound to keep me as long as I behaved myself and showed willingness and ability to pay. It was unfortunate, for she rose to a towering height of rage, avowing her intention of sacrificing all she possessed in the world rather than break her Sabbath rule.

Well, I am a man of peace, and have a certain amount of self-control, so I left the house, caught an earlier train and found most comfortable quarters at Halifax. But wasn't it funny?

CHAPTER VIII

HOSPITALITY

CHAPTER VIII

HOSPITALITY

HOSPITALITY, as generally practised in the three kingdoms, is a very delightful thing, but to the lecturer it is apt to be deadly, unless indeed he is churlish and refuses to reciprocate at all to the kindness shown him. Occasionally, of course, one meets with that most objectionable person whose only reason for giving you an invitation is that you may amuse his or her guests and incidentally shed lustre upon your host as being able to catch such a lion and induce him to roar to order. Happily such folks are rare and are becoming rarer, yet still many lecturers have a well-founded fear of being " entertained within an inch of their lives," and make it a rule to refuse all invitations, preferring to go to an hotel where they can have what they like to eat, go to bed when they like, and get up ditto without fear of putting anybody out or appearing faddish.

I cannot help feeling glad though that I never reached that stage, for I cherish the most delightful memories of all my hosts and hostesses, save two or three, and those only during the South African War, when some of the best and most truthful of men seemed to lose their heads and forget what the truth was, deeming any falsehood believable if it would blacken the character of men who were giving their lives for their country. I certainly did have some bad times with those people, and have had to leave the company to avoid speaking my mind, but I hope that will soon all be forgotten now.

What I chiefly prize about the hospitality which I received is the numbers of good friends, not ephemera, but real friends that I made. I have gone into a house one day and left it the next, having in the meantime made friends whom I can never cease to love while I live and who I feel humbly grateful to think will never cease to love me until they can love no longer. But of all the hospitality I ever enjoyed the quaintest was at Rishton, a suburb of Blackburn, and the manner of it was as follows. I was lecturing at Blackburn in the Town Hall, and on arrival went to the principal hotel with the secretary of the society who met me at the station. There, however, I could only get a bathroom to change in, for they were full, and my friend sent a man round with my bag to another hotel, assuring me that I should be all right there.

After the lecture the secretary invited me to spend an hour at the club, and as I felt fresh I readily consented. There I was introduced to a number of genial clubmen, and the time flew rapidly by until one of those present said :

" I don't want to break up this happy gathering, but I understand Mr. Bullen's staying at the ——, and if he doesn't go now he'll get shut out. It's eleven o'clock, and they're mighty particular."

I rose at once and began to shake hands, when one of the members said nonchalantly :

" Mr. Bullen isn't stopping at the ——, he's stopping with me. George, go over to the —— and ask for Mr. Bullen's bag ; tell 'em I sent you."

There was some little, very little, palaver over this, but I laughed and said I was quite happy whichever way it was, and so we settled down again. It was something past two and only a few of the members remained when my host said cheerily :

" Now, Mr. Bullen, if you're quite ready, don't let me hurry you, I think we'll be getting home."

I rose with haste and professed my perfect readiness to go, indeed I had been wondering slightly how much longer this club séance was going to last. My host then shouted :

" George, call a hansom ! An' see what sort of a night it is, won't ye ? "

Anon George returned, having got a hansom, and the information that it was raining in torrents. Bah, what did that matter? It was dry inside the cab, and although I did feel some qualms about the driver being out in that downpour through four dark miles, I was not in a pessimistic mood, neither was my friend. So we bumped along, chatting gaily, until suddenly my friend smote his knee and uttered a resounding exclamation. Naturally I enquired what had bitten him. After anxiously feeling in all his pockets he replied :

" I've left my key in my office in Manchester, my family are at Bournemouth, and the old woman who does for me goes home at nine o'clock. Funny thing, won't it be, if I can't get into my own house ? "

I made some banal reply, but even this was not sufficient to disturb my optimistic humour, and soon we were both laughing heartily at the episode. Meanwhile the horse plugged steadily on, and at last drew up outside the gate of a fine house. The rain was, if anything, worse, but out jumped my friend, bidding me stay where I was in the dry. I think I should have stayed there anyhow, for with all my good feelings I did not see how I could help matters by getting wet. After quite a long absence my friend returned to report that he had tried every possible door and window within reach only to find them all securely fastened. And the only thing to do now was to drive a mile further to the village where the old caretaker lived, rouse her up, get the key from her, and come back.

I acquiesced cheerfully, making no comment on my friend's saturated condition but thinking ruefully of the poor cabman from whom we had not yet heard. When we arrived at the old lady's house and while my friend was battering at her door to the consternation of the neighbourhood, I looked at my watch and found that it was 3.15. And I softly chuckled to myself until I thought of the poor fellow in the dickey. However, my friend got his key—I heard it fall from an upper window on to the pavement—returned to the cab, and we again started for home. The only reference to his condition made by my friend was that he felt as if he'd been in swimming, but he didn't care, he rather enjoyed the adventure.

At last we reached his door and gained access without further trouble, he giving the cabby a big drink of whisky and I hope paying him well. He then made some coffee on the gas-stove and after we had drunk it we scurried to bed just as the clock struck four. Yet, in spite of that, he was up at seven, got breakfast ready, and we caught the Manchester train at about 8.30, none the worse, as far as I was concerned.

As a contrast to this, let me set off an amazing experience I had in the brave West Country. I was booked to lecture at Plymouth on a certain date, and as I was visiting a relative at Crewkerne some days previously, I was taking my father down with me. A lady wrote to me—and a most charming letter it was—offering the hospitality of her house during my stay in Plymouth, but as I was to have my father's company I regretfully refused, telling her why. A few posts later a letter arrived from her saying that her husband had been suddenly ordered off to Egypt by his doctor and in consequence she would be unable to receive me. But she placed her house and servants and carriage at my disposal, begging me to bring my father and not only to treat the place as if it were my own as regarded us two, but to give entertainment to as many friends as I liked. Indeed she stipulated that I should give at least one dinner-party !

Well, what could I say to such a princely offer as this ? Only accept it gratefully, and in due course father and I arrived at the Great Western Station to find a beautiful carriage and pair awaiting us. We were driven to a stately house on the Hoe and received by the housekeeper with the assurance that in accordance with her instructions she would spare no pains to keep us comfortable. Nor did she. Never can I forget the splendour of that dinner-party, all the guests being friends of my hostess, or the agony of my father who having against my advice loaded up with sandwiches and cake at the five o'clock tea was unable to touch a slice of the noble turkey he carved so well at the head of the table.

I need hardly say that our stay of two days there was all too brief for me, but business called me away, and I had to go. But now that I feel elated when I have eaten one egg and two small slices of toast for my breakfast, I often think of that board spread for us two the morning we left. A noble uncut ham, an untouched glazed tongue, cooked on the premises, and innocent of any tin or glass, half a dozen eggs, a huge brawn, a great jar of Devonshire cream—it was a banquet for a boarding school, and the sight of it almost satisfied our healthy hunger. That was an episode to be remembered, yea, to carry with me. as Kipling says, " to the hungry grave."

It has often given me much food for wondering thought, this practice of hospitality which is carried to a length of which I had never before dreamed. For instance, I have known of quite fierce competition between two families for the honour (?) of putting me up for one night only, and in some cases the matter has only been settled by my consenting to dine in one house and sleep in another. It was always my practice on revisiting a place to stay with the same hosts, if it were convenient for them to have me ; indeed, I always had a standing invitation to do so, but on several occasions I have received letters from other parties, informing me that they had been in negotiation with my former hosts, and had succeeded in inducing them to allow the writers to entertain me this time ! And, do what I would, the thought would assert itself, How pleasant it is to be thus sought after, but why ? I have never found any definite answer.

But several times I have heard rumours to the effect that some lions are not at all easy to cater for. Apropos of that, I remember reading in an American skit upon William Elbert Hubbard, the eccentric genius who founded the Roycroft Brotherhood of Aurora, New York, that upon being offered a sandwich by his trembling hostess, he threw back his mane and said loftily, " It is ten dollars extra if I eat."

Then, without another word, he stalked from the room, and presently there was heard a crash, he had flung a chambermaid downstairs. Humbly asked why, he replied in effect, " It is my humour; let no one question me." Now this is obviously only a caricature, yet I have heard tales which I could not refuse to credit of public men retiring to bed after luncheon with a bottle of whisky; this in a temperance family too! And of a man who is an exceedingly prominent Nonconformist minister who treated his host and hostess with far less courtesy than was due to any hotel-keeper, refusing to eat with them or associate with anybody during his stay, save his secretary, who was accommodated in the same house.

It hardly seems credible that such practices should, not to say endear a man to his hosts, but admit of his being ever entertained again, yet so strangely are people constituted, that behaviour of that kind is condoned and excused as being the hall-mark of genius. On the same principle I suppose as the being possessed of the poetical faculty is held by some to excuse a man from behaving with either cleanliness, decency, sobriety or honesty. Perhaps then it was because I always felt grateful to my hosts and endeavoured to give them as little trouble as possible, while making myself as agreeable as I knew how to be, that I have so many happy recollections of hospitality received.

Once, indeed, my host failed me through no fault of his own, I am sure, although the letter he wrote telling me of his sudden forced departure for London did not reach me until some time after the trouble. The lecture was at Abergwynfi, South Wales, and I arrived there in the gloom of a winter evening, amid a drizzling rain. A less inviting place I have never seen, for the station seemed to end in a black wall of rock, and nothing could be seen around but the grimy cañon along which we had come. Enquiry at the station whether anyone was waiting for anybody only elicited a stare and a curt " no." Further enquiries presently as to whether I could find a hotel and where, brought the stationmaster, who told me of two, and directed me to them.

So I climbed the steep, muddy stairs into the black, foul road, and after a tiring drag, with my heavy bag, of a few hundred yards, I reached a public-house, crammed with drunken miners, who were making a tremendous noise. This surprised me, for I had always thought of the Welsh miner as a quiet man, except in religious fervour, and certainly given to temperance. However, I pushed through the reeking crowd, and enquired at the bar if I could have a room. No ! they had no rooms to let, used to have two, but there was no call for them now. Disheartened, I begged the landlord to let me know

I

where the nearest place was that I could get a room, and he directed me still farther up that hopeless thoroughfare to another place, where they *did* have rooms.

I trudged up there, very wearily, noting as I went the fine Workmen's Institute, where I was to lecture, because of the posters displayed outside and bearing my name. Alas, when I reached the hostelry, which was even more dreary and deplorable looking than the first, but had not so many drunken men in it, I was told that their two spare beds were occupied by two young women with the smallpox, a daughter of the landlord's and a sewing-maid. Of course I lost no time in retreating, and being thus driven, took refuge in the Institute, where I was received by the caretaker with open arms.

I felt at once as if I had accidentally touched the right spring, for my new friend summoned a myrmidon from below, giving him some orders in fluent Welsh, which resulted in the appearance in a very few minutes of a robust man whom I took to be a superior workman or foreman of sorts, but who could not do enough for me. He took me to his home, apologising volubly all the way, and in a very short time his good wife had loaded the little kitchen table with tea, toast, cake, jam and sardines, to all of which I did as much justice, I hope, as was reasonable.

At my suggestion of changing into dress clothes

he turned a puzzled, appealing look upon his wife, and a brief colloquy in Welsh passed between them. Then he said that he hoped I would not trouble to change, for as it was the first time they had ventured upon a lecture or address in English, nobody would expect it. And would I please come along to the Institute and meet the committee? I rose with alacrity, and together we marched up the muddy street towards that building.

The strains of a brass band in the distance saluting my ears, I made some trivial remark about it, to which he replied :

"Oh, yes. I quite forgot to ask you, do you mind the band playing for a few minutes before you begin —by way of introduction like? You see, they've offered, and they're very keen—they do it all for love, and we don't like to discourage them."

Well, what could I do but acquiesce with as much appearance of heartiness as I could muster, though I did begin to wonder whither this affair was tending. But we now met the committee, all working men, who greeted me with enthusiasm, and did their best to make me feel welcome, although the English that some of them spoke was quaint ; and we chatted on until that band played itself in and stopped all conversation. The leader ranged his merry men on the stage behind the sheet, and as the clock struck eight the band burst into a triumphal march. Merciful powers, may I never have such an experience again! Every executant, especially big drum, was determined that his instrument should be heard, no matter what happened, and there were thirty of them! I felt as if the drums of my ears would burst, but feared to offend by going out.

Still, I hoped that the uproar would be brief, indeed, I had been told of ten minutes as the limit. Alas, no! Though their faces were crimson and streamed with sweat, they felt no fatigue, and they clashed, blared and banged on until a quarter to nine, forty-five minutes. There was a hubbub of Welsh congratulations, after which I bowed to the leader of the band (his instrument was the bombardon), and said without emphasis, " Thank you so much." Then I went before the sheet, there being no chairman.

The hall was packed, 600 I should think being present, and of them at least 590 were miners. Not a sound was heard, every face was filled with blank amazement. Not being used to such a reception, I was a bit daunted, but plunged in and talked my best for an hour and a quarter. Still not a sound nor a movement, until one of the committee went before the screen and said something in Welsh, upon which the hall emptied, noisily, it is true, but in most orderly fashion. On joining the committee I expressed a fear that I had not pleased my audience, but my host of teatime hastened to assure me that my efforts were beyond praise.

"Only," he said, "you must remember that very few of the chaps understand English!"

And then, indeed, I was filled with admiration for their good behaviour. To sit and listen to unintelligible explanations of pictures representing something they had never even dreamed of before,—sit for seventy-five minutes and make no protest, then go out in such orderly fashion,—well, it spoke volumes for their characters in the direction of self-restraint.

"Now, sir," broke in my kind guardian again, "if you will come along with us to Blaengwynfi, we have found you a hotel there. This village has no public accommodation at all."

Of course I signified my delighted acquiescence. What else could I do? But I hoped it was not very far, and I was at once assured that it was less than a mile. So we strolled, about eight of us, my bag being carried by one of the party, and soon arrived at the hotel, where I was solicitously attended to in the matter of food, and given quite a decent room. My meal over, I was invited to join my committee, who were evidently out for the evening. Well, what a gay crowd it was, to be sure. They sang and they drank and they smoked—the eleven o'clock rule having been suspended for their benefit apparently, until at about midnight I begged off, and retired to my bedroom. But as it was next to the room in which were the revellers, it was long before I got to sleep, though I have no idea when the merry party broke up.

Next day, however, I found that my bill had been paid, and that everybody was delighted with my behaviour and with the evening generally. Also I found a good train from a station almost opposite to the hotel, and passed away from the district never to visit it again, but to bear it in memory all my life.

CHAPTER IX

HOSPITALITY—*continued*

CHAPTER IX

HOSPITALITY—*continued*

WHILE I am upon this subject of hospitality, I may as well say what I really believe, that as far as my experience goes—and I am fully aware that it does not go very far—I give the palm for knowing how to be really hospitable to my own countrymen, with a slight reservation in favour of the Scotch. But first of all it is necessary to define exactly what I mean by hospitality. Let me say that I am considering it entirely from the point of view of the lecturer. Of the man or woman who has made a long journey, involving very likely all sorts of trying inconveniences, in order to fulfil an engagement to entertain some hundreds of people for a couple of hours or less, and whose first duty is to those people, his employers for the time being.

When a local magnate invites a lecturer to accept his hospitality during the lecturer's stay, he should remember what the lecturer's business is, and that he has very likely to deliver another lecture the following night at some town a long distance away. Most hosts and hostesses do remember this, and act accordingly ; some few, a very few, act as if the lecturer simply came to entertain them and their guests, and had no other business in life. They are not hospitable in the present sense, if, indeed, they are in any other. No one has a right to ask a lecturer to stay with him unless he has the means to make such a public servant comfortable ; no one should act as if the lecturer would be homeless for the night if they do not give him a shelter, unless indeed there be no place of public entertainment in the town, or means of getting out of the town after the lecture.

For it should always be remembered that while lecturers are prepared to put up with a good deal of inconvenience and fatigue in the course of their business, it is not hospitable to add to their burdens in those directions. But perhaps I shall better explain by giving an example of what I mean by an ideal host, an actual experience of course, since fiction finds no place in these pages.

I was booked to lecture in a quiet town not far from Edinburgh, and a gentleman wrote to me some time before, offering me hospitality during my stay, and asking me from what direction I should be coming, and at what time I proposed to arrive. I replied that I should be coming from Glasgow, where I had been staying for a few days with a friend, and that I could come when it would be most convenient for him. He appointed a time to meet him at his club in Glasgow, where I changed and dined with him, then we drove to the station. I made to get my ticket, but he stopped me, saying :

" We have a system of ' guest ' tickets in Scotland, Mr. Bullen, and here is yours," putting the piece of pasteboard into my hand. Of course we travelled first-class, and at our arrival were met by my host's carriage and pair. A happier time I never spent than with him and his amiable family, but I was never *entertained*, I was one of themselves without duties. On the day I was to leave my host took me into his den, and said gravely :

" Mr. Bullen, I pay my servants well on the understanding that none of my guests are to be taxed in tips. You will greatly oblige me, then, if you will refrain from giving any money to anyone in my service. I ask this as a personal favour."

And having ascertained that my next visit was to be to Hawick, my " guest " ticket was made available to that place, I was driven to the station, accompanied by my hostess, and sent upon my way feeling particularly happy. Now I must hasten to say that such treatment is not, could not be, expected everywhere by me or anybody else. But what a contrast to the behaviour of the man who invites you over an undecipherable signature to be his guest at the Laurels, Edgbaston, say, and leaves you to find your way there at the cost of an expensive cab fare, has nobody to greet you when you arrive, invites ten or a dozen people to dinner, at which you are expected to entertain his guests, and after your return, fagged, from your lecture, expects you to entertain a roomful of people until midnight! I needn't go on. For, as I say, such people are very rare, but I am sure they are the cause of many lecturers declining all offers of hospitality whatever.

Not quite so bad as the gentleman I have just sketched was a preparatory schoolmaster for whom I lectured once. The time of the lecture and the distance from London both made it possible for me to catch a train from home which gave me an opportunity not to be missed, for at that time my nights at home during the winter were very few, and therefore precious. So upon hiring my cab at the station I made arrangements for it to call for me after the lecture, and thus satisfactorily fixed for my return I went on gaily through a very jolly lecture. When I had finished the headmaster advanced upon me, and taking my arm, said:

"Come on, Mr. Bullen, dinner is all ready, and I am sure you must want it, I do."

"I'm sorry to say that meals are to me only a necessary evil," I replied, "but, apart from that, I have ordered my cab to catch the London train, and I see I must be off at once if I am to do so."

"Oh, nonsense," he snapped. "It's absurd for you to talk about returning to London to-night. You mustn't do it."

"Very sorry," I persisted, "but my plans are all made, and my people are expecting me. Had you intimated to me beforehand that you would expect me to stay the night, I should then have told you that I could not under the circumstances."

"Well, all I can say is, that if I had known I certainly would not have engaged you. I don't care twopence for the lecture; it was the yarn afterwards that I was looking forward to, and I am extremely disappointed."

Now there was a nice state of affairs! I did the only thing I felt possible—bade him good night, and got into my cab, feeling very angry at what I thought was the perversity of the situation, and leaving my would-be host doubtless very angry at what he considered to be *my* perversity. It is perhaps unnecessary to add that I never got another engagement at that particular school.

Speaking of cabs being retained for the homeward journey reminds me of a wretched experience I had once in Surrey. I was engaged to lecture at a preparatory school, the headmaster of which was a most kindly, courteous gentleman. He warned me some time before I came that the school was six miles from the nearest station, that I must engage a cab to wait and bring me back, the lecture being arranged so that I should have ample time to dine and return to catch a train somewhere about 10.50. But when I was all ready to depart the cabman could not be found—and by the time he did turn up, it was obvious that things were being cut rather fine. And so I told him, but he only replied nonchalantly that there was "plenty of time," and did not hasten one bit. Two or three times on the way I tried to liven him up, but he took no notice, and we arrived at the station to find the train gone. A belated porter came up and gave me the information that the next train was about midnight, due at Waterloo about 1 a.m., and then my cabman said, "How long's she ben gone?"

I am glad to say that I do not remember what I said then. I know it was copious and bitter, but it was utterly lost on the cabman, who simply turned and drove off, leaving me to wait about on a bitter January night in a fireless waiting-room or on a windswept platform until the coming of the last train. I arrived at my hotel in London chilled to the marrow at 1.30 a.m., and owe it to my extraordinary immunity from chills and colds that I did not have a bad bout of illness.

But to return to this matter of hospitality. Taking it all round, I am convinced that there is none so perfectly acceptable to a lecturer at any rate as that in England and Scotland. Irish hospitality is warm, effusive and well meant, but it is too casual, there are too many discrepancies. These can be made fun of, and indeed enjoyed by the young and vigorous, but to the middle-aged, who are none too strong, they are apt to be trying. Such as, for instance, a peat fire in your bedroom on a bitter winter night, which only smoulders and smokes, and gives not the slightest heat. And then to find your pyjamas in the bed wrapped round a leaking hot-water bottle, which has made it necessary to perch precariously upon one edge of the bed, in order to keep dry, but, of course, entailing the destruction of sleep.

But I am in honour bound to say that although I have enjoyed the hospitality of several hundreds of families in this United (as yet) Kingdom of ours, I could count my experiences that were unpleasant on the fingers of one hand, so well is the virtue understood and carried out. In the United States, where I once had a lecture tour, I was never offered hospitality, beyond a meal, but once. And if that once was a fair sample of the custom of the country in that direction, I am very glad. For both my host and hostess regarded me as their property, bound to go through certain performances as a sort of return for my entertainment; and when I jibbed they were immensely surprised. They seemed to think that addressing Boards of Trade, attending Clam Bakes, and speaking pieces from my books to a drawing-room packed with guests invited for the purpose, ought to please me beyond measure, and that all arrangements of the kind might be made without any reference to me or my personal affairs. I am quite willing to believe, however, that such hospitality

may be exceptional. Anyhow, I do not want, as
Martin Ross has it, to be " entertained within an
inch of my life."

Only once in Australia and New Zealand was I
given hospitality—I beg pardon, twice ; but as
both cases were exceptional, and the pleasure they
gave me of the deepest and most lasting kind, I will
say no more about them here. As far as I am concerned, hospitality in Australasia and America has
been non-existent for me, for the exceptions which
I have quoted only go to prove this rule. And now
I must close this chapter, not, indeed, that my matter
on the subject is exhausted, but because—well,
because I want to get on to the burning topic of
hotels. And this is a discursive yarn at best, its only
virtue, as far as I can see, being its absolute truth-
fulness. So we will get on, if you please, to a subject
that is of the deepest interest to all travellers, but
especially to those who travel to earn a living, and
to whom hotel charges are a most serious item.

CHAPTER X

HOTELS

K

CHAPTER X

HOTELS

MY first experience of hotels goes back to 1879, when I arrived in Belfast as a seaman before the mast, and was invited by my good friend, George Hunter, a gentleman who for motives of economy had worked his way home with us before the mast, to dine with him at the Eglinton and Winton Hotel. I was staying at the Sailors' Home at the time, the best, by the way, that I ever did stay in, but as we had not yet been paid off, my wardrobe was not strictly according to shore ideas. I had a good coat and waistcoat, but I had to wear a pair of moleskin trousers. They were milk-white with energetic washing, but they must have looked funny, for I remember a hilarious commercial after dinner asking me if I was one of the Welsh miner-heroes (there had been a terrific colliery accident in North Wales not long before, attended by the usual heroic endeavours to save life).

I also remember that the food seemed to me the finest of which I had ever dreamed, but then I was fresh from five months of forecastle grub. That, however, was no excuse for my lifting the last cauli-flower out of the dish proffered me, even if it was no bigger than a duck egg. To a seaman fresh from five months' utter privation of vegetables, it was but a mouthful, but something of the enormity of my offence was borne in upon me when the waiter (he was an Irishman) proffered the empty dish to my neighbour.

"Get me some cauliflower," said that gentleman promptly, not without a stern glance at my plate.

"There's no more," replied the waiter, and the silence that ensued was thick enough to cut. For four persons had not been served with cauliflower. Yet, British fashion, no man complained, and the dinner proceeded in grim silence. And I felt bewildered, for my senses told me that I had not been greedy, and yet I could not help feeling also that I had annexed the cauliflower of four diners.

Two years afterwards I arrived at Dundee, and remembering my former experiences, went to a hotel for the one night I was to stay there. And when I sat down to the laden table and the waitress placed a 20-lb. joint of cold roast beef before me to help myself, the hungry months behind me faded away, and I fed blissfully. They only charged me 2s. for my meal, but I am sure they were heavy losers, for I must have eaten over a pound of meat, to say nothing of bread, butter, jam and cake. But

I feel that they could have few such appetites as mine then was to cater for.

It was many years before I was a guest at a hotel again, and then, alas! my appetite had gone. Gone so completely that I did not want any breakfast at any time, and for my principal meal in the middle of the day the smallest quantity of the plainest food. And if that food were tough or badly cooked or unpleasant, I wanted nothing but a piece of bread. This made me fiercely critical of hotel charges. I could not remember that to keep up a great establishment it was necessary to charge a fairly high price, and to cater for people with appetites, not abnormalities like myself, satisfied with a cup of coffee and a slice of bread and butter for breakfast, and fiercely resentful at having to pay 2s. for it.

Nevertheless, it is possible to recognise facts that you cannot alter, and I speedily became passive under the infliction of comfortless splendour and high charges for meals that I couldn't eat. I need hardly say that I never by any chance took a table d'hôte dinner *so* cheap at 5s., or ditto luncheon at 3s. 6d., fulfilling the requirements of the hotel, which threatened a fine of 2s. if I did not take meals in the house, by paying 2s. for a cup of coffee and a slice of bread and butter at breakfast-time. But in Scotland I found attached to every large hotel a restaurant where the food was really excellent; quality, quantity, variety and price being all that one could desire. There I could dine or lunch for about 1s. 6d. as well as I desired, one plate always serving me, always being sufficient. I know that some people on reading this will esteem me mean, but I am really not so, only I do hate having to pay for a succession of dishes whereof I can only eat one.

I always found, too, that the better the hotel the more moderate were the charges as compared with second- and third-rate places, with the vile old system of charging for attendance, which benefits nobody but the proprietor, and means that you have to pay twice or the attendants get no tips. It is not a bit too emphatic to call the system vile, for these places hire their servants for a few shillings a month, on the distinct understanding that they, the servants, make up for their scanty wages by tips, which the customer has already paid in the bill. Nothing could well be more paltry, dishonest and irritating than such a system, for even the seaside lodging-house keepers' extras are not nearly so annoying. Fortunately the better class of hotels have abolished the system altogether. You know what you have to pay, and even if you feel that the old extras are added in, that is not half so irritating as the old system.

One of the strangest things that I have noted in my hotel experience is the inferiority of the Temperance Hotel. There must be some exceptions, of course, or how can the popularity of the huge Cranston

Hotels be explained; but, speaking generally, so far as my experience goes, in a temperance hotel, food, attendance, accommodation, and civility are all far below what is obtainable in licensed hotels. I do not pretend to explain it, but I have known many men who were total abstainers who shuddered at the thought even of going to a temperance hotel. Is it, I wonder, anything to do with the fact that all temperance drinks are vile, thirst-provokers and stomach-destroyers. Except perhaps water, and even water in satisfying quantity is not good for the middle-aged. It is a puzzle which I leave to wiser heads than mine.

Then there is the Commercial Hotel. If you are a commercial, nothing can well be better. The food is of the best, the charges are reasonable, and the tips exceedingly modest. But if you are not one of the knights of the road, you are in parlous case. The worst room in the house, the almost undisguised scorn of the attendants, the quite undisguised dislike of the guests are yours without asking. The very last hotel I stayed in was a Temperance Commercial Hotel, which outside looked like a large and charming family villa—but my room was positively filthy, with black rotten paper hanging off the walls, a bed apparently made of dumplings, no fire-place, and for light a feeble gas-jet in a remote corner, where it only served to show what a den the room was. I asked for a fire to be made in my room, for the night was bitterly cold, and the two public rooms downstairs were full of tobacco smoke, which I cannot breathe for coughing, but I was told that it was impossible, as there was no fire-place—I had not then seen the room. Why did I go there? Well, the room was taken for me by the secretary of the society I was to lecture for—I attach no blame to him—and when I found out it was too late, in my weak condition, to go anywhere else. But this was in a town of 200,000 inhabitants in the North of England.

Let it be understood once for all that I dislike hotels as necessary evils, but that my sense of justice compels me to admit that one may be made comfortable in a gigantic caravanserai where it would seem impossible for the personal element to have any chance to express itself, and, conversely, that one may be made abjectly miserable in a very small hotel where it might naturally be thought that the proprietor would make it his sole business to see that his guests were comfortable. Management is the keynote of it all, but even that is powerless against other advantages such as position, want of competition, etc. Most gratefully do I bear tribute to one splendid characteristic of all the great hotels owned by the Midland Railway Company—the quality and get-up of their bed-linen. It must be an education in comfort to some people, wealthy folks, too, who stay in them; for I can honestly say that in no private house, however costly in its appointments, have I ever enjoyed contact with such sheets and pillow-slips as in any Midland hotel that I have ever stayed in, and I think I have sampled them all.

For sheer magnificence, which does not always mean comfort by any means, the Great Scottish Railway Hotels are easily first of all the hotels I know, which, of course, does not mean anything of the " Carlton " or " Ritz " type. Why is it, I wonder, that Edinburgh and Glasgow can and do so easily excel our great metropolis in railway stations and hotels ? The finest terminus in London is a mere undistinguished siding compared with Waverley, Princes Street or Central Stations ; nor, although St. Pancras Hotel is architecturally very fine, does it compare with the castellated splendour of the North British Hotel at Waverley.

But if only they could be found now I would infinitely prefer the old English inns, with their plain roast and boiled, chops and steaks and simple vegetables. Even now may be found in some of them, daily, alas ! growing fewer, the same high quality of meat and vegetables, and the same almost reverent care in their simple preparation, a preparation that did not depend upon some mysterious sauce to give flavour to the meat, but brought out all the delicious qualities that the unsophisticated food itself possessed. Unfortunately, even a wayside inn will now give you a *menu* written in amazing French, and dishes more amazing still, concocted by people who doubtless would have been good at plain boiled or roast, but who make an awful mess of a ragout, an entrée, or a fricassee. Still, as they would very justly retort, these unholy mix-ups are asked for and expected by their patrons, who having eaten heartily of them, go away and growl that it is only in France that you can get food decently cooked.

But I am reminded that tastes differ. I only wish that folks would practise toleration in food matters as well as religion. To the latter we are all coming—even the Catholics will, I understand, allow you to do and believe anything you like, so long as you say you are a Catholic, go to your duty once in a while and pay up—sure that's all easy. Then why shouldn't men admit that what is one man's meat is another man's poison, and let it go at that? They don't, though. One of the most frequent remarks made to me during my lecturing days by hostesses was:

" Now, Mr. Bullen, tell me just what you would like before you lecture and what afterwards. I only want to know, because I am aware how necessary it is that a lecturer should have just what food agrees with him and at the time he needs it."

My invariable reply that whatever the family were taking for dinner would suit me admirably, and that I wanted nothing after a lecture, was always received with polite astonishment—I will not say incredulity, but certainly there was conveyed to me an idea that I could not be sincere, or, if so, that I must be a totally different subject from the majority of lecturers and other public men. As far as lecturers go, I hasten to say that I do not think that any with whom I am acquainted are difficult to please or at all *tête montée*. Still, you never know. But public men! Ah, there you have me. They may be a fearful sort of wild-fowl to entertain, especially if they have only recently arrived.

Alas, I am wandering far away from my chapter heading, which is hotels. And no hotel in which I ever stayed was at all concerned about anything but what I chose to order and pay for. And if that was served as I wanted it, well, glory! all was as happy as could be. But of all the infernal places on earth to stay at, defend me from a hotel whose iron-bound rules forbid any guest to have anything in the nature of food or drink except at certain stipulated hours. These dens, I can call them nothing else, flourish in the United States, where the democracy submit to more tyranny than any place outside of Turkey. Shall I ever forget an occasion when I lay groaning with acute indigestion in a hotel in Chatauqua Lake summer resort? I was parched with thirst, knotted up with pain, empty as a drum, but knew I dared not eat. At last (it was Sunday morning about ten o'clock), at something like the thirteenth ring, a youth came and slammed my door open.

" Waal ! " he said. " Waat ye want ? "

I looked at him with glazed eyes, and said faintly:

" A little milk and soda, please, as soon as you can."

" Ye cain't have nothin' till dinner-time ! " with an air of finality perfectly Rhadamantine.

That did me good. I sat up in bed, the excruciating pain temporarily forgotten, and enquired :

" In heaven's name, why can't I have a milk and soda ? "

His answer was concise, and closed the discussion in one direction.

" Bekase th' manager's gone out, an' he has th' key of the kitchen, an' nothin' k'n be served till he comes back at one o'clock."

Then I recognised, as they say, what I was up against, and I pleaded hard. But it was of no avail, I had to wait until one o'clock, and then—while milk could be had in plenty, there was no soda ! So I was as badly off as ever, for milk alone in the state I was enduring was so much poison to me. I could not understand it, nor can I now. So difficult is it to understand that I never expect to be believed when I tell the following story. The next evening I was to lecture in the auditorium, a huge, umbrella-shaped building set apart for the purpose, and before the lecture I sought the janitor, and endeavoured to enlist his sympathies in the matter of soda and milk, at any rate. I assumed that he would be as surprised as I was that soda was not to be got in so highly civilised a place, and apparently I was right, for he responded at once with a snort of contempt for the fools, as he called them, and assured me that he would get me my milk and soda in two ticks. I gave him a dollar, and in less than ten minutes he returned with a jug of milk and a pound of washing soda ! I know I can never be believed, but I declare that this is true.

But I can honestly say that I never but once had as good a meal anywhere in America, and I always stayed at the best hotels I could find (private houses I only know of two), as any workman can get in London for eightpence. The exception was at President Roosevelt's table at Oyster Bay. We had lamb cutlets, potatoes and cauliflower, with rice pudding to follow, and it was all delicious. It made me feel quite home-sick. But it was unique. I never got it again. In Canada it is practically the same, though I will gladly admit of an exception in the case of the Château Frontenac at Quebec, and, oh, yes, there is the "Empress" at Victoria, Vancouver Island. The "Prince George" at Toronto was better than any United States Hotel I ever stayed in, and quite equal to any English hotel I know, but that is not saying a great deal.

As to the food in the trains, it makes me shudder to think of it. I really cannot say all I know to be true about it, for fear of being thought extravagantly biased, but in very truth I nearly starved on the C.P.R. I have had lamb (so called) black and tough as leather, lake trout that was positively putrid, and—but there, it is useless to make a list. When I say that I was reduced to eating baked beans and bread at every meal, and that I lost a stone in weight in one month, I best convey the straits to which I was reduced. To my mind the strangest thing about the whole business was that when we got on board the boat to go from Vancouver to Victoria, although presumably the catering arrangements were the same, the food was excellent. I could not wish for anything better, but I tried in vain to discover any reason for the difference.

As a matter of actual experience I never realised how good and comfortable a place a hotel could be until I went to Australia seven years ago. During my previous visits as a lad and a young man I had learned to love and admire Australasia, because of its lavish distribution of food at low prices. It will hardly be believed, but it is a fact that when I went to Lyttelton in 1878 a carpenter could earn 15s. per day, and could get board and lodging for 15s. per week, the board meaning three huge meals with meat, vegetables, bread, and pastry, also tea, and coffee and beer. Sixpence was the ordinary workman's price for a meal in an eating-house at all the ports in Australasia, and better, more copious meals it would be hard to find. But then Australasia had not, and never has, as far as I know, handed over her food supply to a meat trust, and thereby bound her people, no matter what their station in life may be, to eat whatever garbage Chicago chooses to dole out to them.

Still, those early experiences of mine were only of eating-houses; I never stayed in a hotel, of course. But on this last visit, after I had become thoroughly well acquainted with hotels in Great Britain, America and the Continent, I stayed in hotels all over Australasia, and I firmly believe as a result of that experience that they can safely, or that they could safely, be spoken of generally as the best hotels in the world. But here arises a small difficulty. Every little pub, no matter how small, ordinary or low class, calls itself a hotel, and strangers are apt to be misled by the title. Still, titles are always misleading people everywhere, so the hotel business in Australasia cannot claim any monopoly in misnaming.

What I wish to point out from actual experience, and as entirely unbiased as any opinion can ever be, is that in Australasia, as in no other country that I have ever visited, may be found, in the great cities as in remote country places, hotels which will give the traveller an abundance of excellent food well and plainly cooked, with a great variety of beautiful vegetables also in plentiful quantities, such as a man would expect in his own comfortable home. Not only so, but the tariffs charged were extremely reasonable, affording the strongest possible contrast to Canada, where I believe the hotel charges are the highest, and the treatment generally the worst, in the world. But these were not the only matters I saw to admire in Australasian hotels. In all my experience of them I was never charged anything beyond the agreed daily tariff—there were no extras. And I was always served with early morning tea and afternoon tea, while for those who liked to eat between meals there was food at 11 a.m., no table laid, and again at about 10 p.m. And baths were looked upon as a necessary of life, and never charged for. Nor were there any tips.

Now I am perfectly well aware that hotel keepers everywhere else, especially in my own beloved country, will, if they believe these statements (a very large "if," by the way), declare that such a procedure on their part would only spell bankruptcy. Well, of course, I do not know their business, but I may be permitted to disbelieve such a statement entirely. In Australasia wages are higher, rent is higher, food is certainly no cheaper, and hotel keepers certainly not philanthropists, yet the thing is done, and done as I have said.

CHAPTER XI

CHAIRMEN

CHAPTER XI

CHAIRMEN

THIS ought to be a very long chapter, in spite of the fact that it has been done supremely well before. But I have not read M. Paul Blouet's able work, nor have my experiences been his, so that I approach this very interesting part of my subject with a light heart. Let me at the outset declare that I by no means disapprove of chairmen, as so many of my colleagues do. A chairman who knows his business, and confines his share of the proceedings to a few well-chosen sentences, and the appearance of his name on the bills, is a jewel of price, and I have often been very glad to meet him. But I must admit that he is rare, and the difficulty that a secretary is always in when inviting a local celebrity to take the chair at a lecture is his inability to know whether the L.C. will not consider it a part of his functions to make a long rambling speech while the audience is waiting impatiently to hear the lecturer. As for the latter, he doesn't count, of course, but I have often wondered what the chairman would have thought could he have known what was beneath my placidly smiling exterior, as I sat facing the audience, while the hands of the clock crept slowly round. And then the crowning outrage at about 8.25.

" But you don't come to hear me, you come to hear the lecturer, and so I won't stand between you and him any longer. But this I must say." And then another five minutes of vapid twaddle. It is impossible to do justice to such people as that, and still more impossible for a lecturer to realise that there are people who really like that sort of thing. At least one would think so, judging by what they say aloud, but what they think, who can tell ? However, between a chairman of that kind and no chairman at all there is a wide gap, and I cannot say that I ever grew to like the growing practice of expecting the lecturer to walk on the platform and begin his lecture as soon as eight o'clock strikes. And yet there is a further great advantage in this, you miss the absolutely nauseating votes of thanks at the end. What puny-minded person ever devised that method of giving pain to a poor man who has done them no intentional harm, to say nothing of making him and others lose their train very often, I have never been able to ascertain, but he was no friend of mine, whoever he was.

I suppose as I am writing about chairmen I ought to begin with instances where there were none, in order to fulfil modern literary requirements.

Such instances, at any rate, will not take up much time, but I very well remember the first experience I ever had of the system. It was at Moseley or King's Heath or Rotton Park, one of those suburbs of Birmingham, at any rate, which used to be famous for their Institutes, and to which we lecturers used to look forward for a consecutive list of seven or eight engagements. On arrival at the hall I saw no one except a bluff caretaker, who conducted me to a bare room, and brought me a chair. I asked him if there were no officials connected with the place whom I might expect to see before the lecture. He replied that there was no one there except himself and the audience.

"They're in their seats all right," he said; "and if you go on up those stairs when the clock strikes eight, you'll find 'em before you. An' a jolly good audience, too, they are."

"But surely," I demurred, "this isn't usual. Do the lecturers never see anybody but the caretaker? And who do I look to for my fee?"

"Oh!" he laughed, "you'll see the treasurer all right after the lecture. But that's eight striking. This way, sir."

I went in the direction indicated, and found myself facing a packed concourse of people, who gave me a rousing cheer. I began my lecture straight away, and was at once on the best possible terms with my audience, so that the hour and three-quarters passed like half an hour. But immediately the lights were turned up the hall began to empty, and by the time I was back in the little bare waiting-room again I think the caretaker and I were almost the only persons left in the building. He advanced towards me with a beaming smile, holding out an envelope, which he said the treasurer had asked him to hand me, because he was in a great hurry to get somewhere else.

" I suppose you can guess what's in it," he murmured, with a grin of pure good-fellowship.

I found it contained my cheque and a note " with the treasurer's compts.," and that was all. Still, although it was amply sufficient, I couldn't help feeling that it was just a little too business-like, and said so. I was not at all surprised to hear that one lecturer who was a very big gun indeed, and whose fee was three times mine, felt himself so slighted, and his dignity so hurt, that upon meeting with similar treatment, he promptly refused to deliver his lecture, and departed as he had come. That, to my mind, was utterly indefensible conduct, punishing as it did a large number of quite innocent people. Besides the folly of it, for the lecturer would without doubt be blamed for non-appearance, and would have no chance of setting his side of the case before the audience.

I must admit, however, that such behaviour towards a lecturer is most unusual, and, in any case, it implies a great compliment, for it assumes that there is no chance of default on the part of the principal figure in the entertainment. But I must get on to the positive side of chairmen, and here I find myself embarrassed with riches. Strangely enough, one of the very last lectures I gave was embittered by an unwise chairman, who should have known better, since he was the pastor of the chapel where the lecture was given. My host, who lived near, had invited a wealthy friend to join us in the drive to the chapel—it was a bitterly cold, foggy night—and on arrival I was asked at what time the carriage should call for us, so as not to keep the coachman or the horse waiting in such inclement weather. Of course I said 9.40, the lecture being announced to begin at eight, and the coachman drove away.

Right here I find that I was just about to do a very worthy gentleman a grave injustice. My chairman was his worship the Mayor, but his functions were usurped by the parson, who led us on to the platform. The proceedings were opened by the parson giving out a long hymn, which was sung right through. Then followed a prayer, which lasted twelve minutes. Then another hymn was sung, and on its completion the pastor gave us an address about nothing in particular, but really, I think, for the pleasure of hearing himself speak. After ten minutes of this he introduced the chairman, who was commendably brief, but still occupied another five minutes. Then we sang another long hymn, after which that irrepressible parson introduced me with a great deal of tiresome eulogy. Eventually I faced the audience at 8.40, the forty minutes having been worse than wasted, for I was fretted almost beyond endurance, and so, I am sure, were many of the audience. I did my best to hurry through the lecture, but with the best will in the world it was 10.5 when I had finished. I am glad to say that I protested to the parson, in the interests of the next lecturer, but he only seemed surprised that anyone should object to what he considered were essential preliminaries. What my host and his guest said I leave to the imagination, my host being especially angry because of his coachman and valuable horse, condemned to endure that bitter fog for over half an hour to no purpose whatever.

Still, I suppose I must be grateful for small mercies in this case, for, owing to the Mayor saying that he must needs leave, we were spared what I am sure would otherwise have been another half-hour's piffle, my undaunted parson being fully wound up to make three or four speeches more. On other occasions I have not been so fortunate. I have always tried my utmost to keep within the limits of an hour and a half, believing, as I firmly do, that more than that must bore an audience, besides rendering some of them liable to lose their trains in many cases. But alas!

I have often found that the persons responsible for the lecture seemed to have no account of time or thought for anybody's convenience, much less comfort. One such occasion I remember with considerable bitterness. The hall was immense, seating over two thousand on one floor, and at the back the people's heads touched the ceiling. It was not ventilated at all, and packed with people, and as many of them had been in their places since 7.30, it may be imagined that the air was pretty thick when I marched on the platform, escorted by eight of the committee. No time was lost by the chairman in getting to work, but he had not been speaking for two minutes before I recognised what I was in for.

I have not the least idea what his speech was about, except that it had nothing to do with my lecture or lecturing in the abstract. After about ten minutes of it the audience began to signify their uneasiness by shuffling their feet, clapping and an occasional " sit down." The chairman, however, held steadily on, raising his voice, as it became necessary, to make it heard above the growing hubbub, until at last there was a veritable pandemonium of noise, and he had to stop. But he waited only until the noise subsided, and then cried :

" Ye can mak' all the noise ye're a mind to. Ah'm goin' ta deliver ma speech if Ah stand here a' neet."

Well ! One would have thought Bedlam had broken loose. The uproar was terrific. I began to wonder what *was* going to happen. But though I hated that chairman violently, I could not help admiring him for his pluck and tenacity. Every one of the seven committee men begged him to sit down, but in vain, and at last, by sheer force of will and lung power, he did finish his speech, at 8.25. It was a fine exhibition of pertinacity, but it did me no good, for I was in momentary dread that the platform would be stormed; so furious had the audience become. But it was nothing short of wonderful to see how, directly the chairman had retired, every one settled down in perfect quiet. I could not have wished for a better hearing. But as soon as I had finished, which I did at ten o'clock, the hall began to empty with much noise of scuffling and chatter. That made no sort of difference to the committee. The chairman at some length called upon Mr. So-and-so to propose a vote of thanks to the lecturer. Eagerly Mr. So-and-so responded, also at some length, and when he had resumed his seat the chairman called upon Mr. Thingumy to second the motion. More speech—I may say that owing to the hubbub in the hall and the " hushing " of the committee, not a word of these addresses was heard, not that it seemed to matter to the speakers—and when the seconder had finished, the motion was put in due form, declared carried, and I was informed that the meeting unanimously thanked me for my address.

I merely bowed. I could not trust myself to speak,

for fear of prolonging the proceedings. By now the hall was nearly empty, but still the dreary business went on—the chairman and lanternist had to be thanked, and, of course, the speaker could not be expected to curtail the speech he had waited so long to deliver. And so the long evening wore on until at 10.45 I emerged from the building, thoroughly weary, and feeling that I had well earned my fee. To many people I know that what I have stated will appear incredible, but I have no interest in stating untruths, even if I would do so, and I hope that no one will think me capable of so doing.

One quaint experience brings a smile even now, although I doubt very much if the chief performer saw any fun in the matter, and I am sure I hope that he was none the worse. Everything was very nice indeed as regards the preliminaries, and I quite fraternised with the secretary, a charming man. But as we were waiting for the chairman he said:

" I ought to warn you, Mr. Bullen, that our chairman is inclined to be a little long-winded. He can't speak for nuts, but he's the mainstay of the society, and most generous, and as all he expects in return is that he shall be chairman, we can't very well refuse. But I'll own that he's a bit of a trial sometimes. Still, you'll overlook that, won't you, seeing matters are as I tell you ? "

I readily assented, more especially when the chairman came in, and I was introduced to him. He was a fine soldierly-looking man, of about sixty-five, I should judge, and though he spoke little, what he did say was full of sense and to the point. Moreover, it was easy to see that he had the welfare of the Lecture Society very much at heart, and was anxious above all things that it should be a success. I was greatly taken with him, so much so, indeed, that I began to feel sure that the secretary was pulling my leg—it seemed impossible that such a man as the chairman seemed to be could be as foolish as the secretary's words implied. However, eight o'clock struck, and we went on the platform, to the usual accompaniment of applause, to which I bowed and sat down.

The chairman then advanced to the front of the platform, and began the most extraordinary speech to which I have ever listened. I was petrified with astonishment, for the man seemed in some mysterious way to have changed. He gave utterance to an incoherent jumble of words, that made me feel dizzy with my attempts to get a clue to their meaning. Not for long, because I soon concluded that there was no meaning, but that left other things entirely unexplained. Evidently the audience were well used to him, for they sat quite still as he rambled on, obviously prepared to endure him as long as they could. And then another fact became evident: not only could the poor man only talk nonsense, but he could not find a place to leave off. And I began to worry myself seriously as the hands of the clock stole round, and still the flood of fortuitous words rolled on.

Then I noticed that the lights were being turned out. The hall was lit by large arc lamps, in pairs, and some unseen friend was switching them off two by two, until only two were left, and they were in such a position that the platform was nearly dark. And suddenly the chairman disappeared! He had fallen off the platform! And the audience applauded frantically, as if it had been a well-rehearsed effect most successfully performed. But, stranger still, the unseen friend switched off the remaining lights, the lanternist flashed on the first picture, and I plunged into my lecture. I never was listened to with more attention, nor have I ever been more appreciated, and the end of the lecture came with a suddenness that surprised me. But there were no votes of thanks, for—I never saw the chairman again. Nor to this day do I know whether his sudden descent from the platform injured him or not, for on my return to the anteroom, fully prepared to condole or excuse, whatever, in fact, seemed indicated, not a word was said by the secretary about the occurrence at all. Not that there was any awkwardness or stiffness about our intercourse, the matter simply wasn't mentioned, that was all. But to this day it strikes me as the funniest as well as the most dramatic ending to a chairman's speech I ever heard of or experienced.

But in this case I was warned, and consequently I did not feel at all annoyed or worried. There was an occasion, not so very long ago, though, when I was both, because in addition to what I suffered, the chairman had previously assured me that he knew nothing about the business, that it was his first time of officiating, and he begged me to tell him just what he should do. I gave him a very candid outline of what I considered to be the duties of a chairman, and he promised me fervently that he would follow my directions implicitly, thanking me heartily for what he was pleased to call my kindness. So I felt very satisfied as I whispered to my host, the pastor of the chapel, what had happened.

It is not, therefore, easy to judge of my disgust and annoyance when after an opening that was a model of what a chairman's address should be, this worthy man slid into an anecdote about his one and only voyage, which had neither point nor wit nor moral, and took twenty-five minutes in the telling. After which the usual wicked insult about not standing between the audience and the lecturer because they all wanted to hear what Mr. Bullen had to tell them. Then the miscreant sat down, at 8.30, and I got up, boiling with indignation, and extremely hard put to it to refrain from telling them that it was impossible for me to go on now. Only my strong sense of justice enabled me to act upon what I always felt to be right, a refusal to punish all the audience for the offence of one man.

By the time the lecture was finished I had recovered my equanimity, and was quite prepared for a long and dreary period of moving, seconding and carrying votes of thanks. But I was not in the least prepared to hear my host, the parson, in moving the vote of thanks, include the chairman, and make a long eulogy of the delightful and most interesting reminiscence they had all enjoyed from the chairman ! So now they were doubly indebted to him, not merely for presiding at that gathering, but for giving them so dramatic, so entertaining, so perfectly charming a description of his own experiences, and he, the parson, earnestly trusted that he, the chairman, would favour them again at the earliest opportunity. Of course after that the chairman could do no less than make another long, rambling speech, in the course of which he repeated himself six times, and I sat simmering. I had acknowledged the vote by a bow, I could not trust myself to speak, but as soon as I got the parson by himself I asked him point-blank what on earth he could have meant by what he said. His reply was somewhat incoherent, but the gist of it was that the goodwill of the chairman was important to their little community, while I didn't matter. They might, and probably would never see me again, and anyhow it was of no consequence what I thought. He put it much nicer than that, but that was the sense of it, and I could not help acknowledging the force of his contention. So we will leave it at that.

Here it suddenly occurs to me that some folks will suppose that because of the few cranks I have endeavoured to sketch, my experiences of chairmen have been almost uniformly unpleasant. Now nothing could well be further from the truth. The chairmen whom I have had the good fortune to meet and to appear on the platform with have been with very few exceptions gentlemen with a perfect conception of their duties to the audience and the lecturer, and it has fairly often fallen to my lot to enjoy the chairman's speech so thoroughly that I have been sorry when he has left off. But I suppose that only throws into higher relief the few cranks about whom I am writing. At any rate, having made my point clear, I hope, I will give a few more instances of chairmen who have made me wish them (or myself) elsewhere.

One gentleman in particular I remember who made me feel desperately uncomfortable, although I am sure that his intentions were as benevolent as he knew how to make them. He told the intent audience such things about me as made me go hot and cold all over. If he could have been believed, I ought never to have been sitting upon that platform, but enstatued in gold and set upon high, clear for all men to see and take pattern by. I was the fine flower not only of a blameless, strenuous and overcoming life, but the quintessence of the best of the age. Never but once have I had to listen to such encomia upon myself, and that was at second-hand in a theological college near Gisborne, New Zealand. A Maori student orated at me, and one of his fellows translated. But that was not so bad, for somehow we all understood that at least ninety per cent must be deducted for rhetoric. This Englishman, however, speaking of me—me who sat suffering there by his side—ransacked all his obviously great reading for tropes and metaphors wherewith to enrich his eulogy of me, with the net result that I never felt more exquisitely uncomfortable.

When at last he had concluded, and I stood up to address my auditors, I began by bewailing not merely my inability to justify the praises of me they had heard, but that of any son of Adam to do so. Yet as nothing on earth is evil unmixed, I had derived some benefit from the exceedingly severe trial through which I had passed, in that I had learned that it was still in my power to blush and feel uneasy at undeserved praise. This was well worth a little inconvenience to learn, for already I had heard as much flattery as any ordinary person could swallow, and had hardly turned a hair. I suppose the long years of buffeting and contumely through which I had passed—for I was over forty years of age before I ever got any praise for anything—had made that

M

sweet incense almost savourless to me when it did come. At any rate, I can safely say that I was so toughened against it that it did me very little harm. I never grew to look for it as my due, and feel slighted if it were not paid.

But this chapter is growing to an inordinate length, and I must, for the sake of appearances, commence a new one, although it will still be upon the topic of chairmen. But I hope in the next chapter to mingle a good deal of praise with what has perhaps appeared like censure or at least sarcasm. It is not really, for I am fully convinced that each of the gentlemen I have described did his level best to fulfil what he conceived to be his duty, and it was only because he had somehow got a wrong idea of what that duty was that he made such obvious blunders.

CHAPTER XII

CHAIRMEN—*continued*

CHAPTER XII

CHAIRMEN—*continued*

ONLY my fixed determination to avoid mentioning names prevents me from giving the title of a noble chairman who filled that office for me in a certain country town. Those of my late colleagues who do me the honour to read these lines will quite understand what I mean when I say that I had not the least idea, although I saw his name on the bills, that the chairman would appear. The trick is a very old one, and so often practised that it ceases to surprise. A good name brings the people, and an apology for his *unavoidable* absence and inability to keep his engagement from some well-known substitute always seems to go down. Therefore I was considerably astonished when the noble individual arrived punctually, accompanied by his lady. He made a most charming introductory speech, lasting barely ten minutes, during which he said many pleasant things, but more especially made it evident that he had carefully read my books, and so got up the subject on which I was to lecture. And after the lecture was over he made another little speech, to which I listened with extreme pleasure. In fact, I have rarely enjoyed anything more than I did this noble gentleman's two addresses, so free were they from fulsome adulation on the one hand, and offensive patronage on the other.

By way of contrast I recall a most unpleasant experience I had in a Congregational church of all places. Now most of my lectures have been given in connection with Nonconformist places of worship, and except that they are rather given to lengthy proceedings at the end, when everybody wants to get away, the lecturer most of all, I must say I have always enjoyed them very much — especially Congregationalists. Some of the other denominations are a bit inclined to be narrow (though that is really personal), but I have always found among the Congregationalists a broadness of toleration and outlook that is very pleasant. It is no easy matter, then, to judge of my surprise when during my lecture at this particular church of which I am speaking, my chairman, who was the pastor, suddenly sprang to his feet and flatly contradicted something I had said. The funny part was that it was really a quotation I made, and the utterance of the chairman was: "Professor So-and-so never said anything of the kind!"

This sudden outburst placed one in a grave difficulty. I had never had a similar experience, and I, of course, did not carry books with me to prove the correctness of my memory. For a few seconds there was an utter silence and considerable nervous tension. Then I said very quietly and distinctly:

"Perhaps the best thing to do under the circumstances, Mr. Chairman, will be to allow the lecture to proceed, and at its close I will endeavour to justify any statements I have made, and answer any of your questions."

The chairman just bobbed up and apologised, saying that he had forgotten himself, and I proceeded. But at the close of the lecture, though I professed my willingness to go freely into the matter, there was no challenging word spoken by the chairman or anyone else, and the matter then dropped, as they say in the House of Lords. But I have often wondered since how far the chairman of a lecture is justified in thus interrupting the lecturer, even when his knowledge of the subject is far greater than that of the speaker. In this case it certainly was not so, but the chairman was fanatic upon the subject of evolution, and he was afraid that I was trying to teach evolution to his congregation by a side-wind.

I had a great deal of fun out of one chairman, who was also my host, a rough jewel, if ever there was one. It was in one of the dingy, dreary Lancashire manufacturing towns, and my host was the Mayor as well as being the biggest mill-owner in the place. He had risen literally from the ranks, and his speech was hardly intelligible to me; also his house, which was small, was so crammed with incongruous rubbish as to be almost uninhabitable, while he and his good wife spoke their minds to me and each other with a frankness that took a little getting used to, as they say.

They were mightily amused at me, principally at my very small appetite. Their table was loaded at meal-times with the most solid food, and I specially remember the hot buttered toast, the hot, greasy cakes, the great dish of fried fish at tea-time, the very thought of that mountain of food gives me indigestion. That, however, is not the point. On the day of my lecture the weather was very bad, and as the time approached for us to go, the rain increased, until it was a regular tropical downpour. His Worship's carriage was at the door, and we scurried into it, very nearly getting drenched in the passage. As soon as we had started I said to his Worship: " It's almost a pity to leave home, isn't it ? There cannot be anybody there on a night like this."

" They'll be all there," he replied sententiously. " The 'all'll be full, you'll see. We don't mind th' weather up 'ere."

I cannot hope to reproduce his Lancashire dialect, so do not try. Indeed, it would be impossible, for most of the time he was quite unintelligible to me, and I had previously prided myself on my ability, not merely to pick up languages, but to assimilate any dialect of my own tongue. Nothing more was said between us, and we duly arrived at the hall, when his Worship at once asked the official who met us at the side door if the audience were in their places,

and was answered by a laconic " Ay ! " We entered
the anteroom on the stroke of eight, and, to my amazement as well as amusement, an official came forward
with the mayoral robes and insignia of office—very
imposing and massive they were too. Truly his
Worship looked a gallant figure as he stalked on to
the platform, and I felt quite insignificant beside
him in my evening dress.

A great shout of welcome went up from the audience
at which I bowed, but his Worship stood stiffly erect,
and then, taking my seat, I stared with utter astonishment at the sight before me. The great hall was
packed from end to end, even to the standing room,
and there was quite a haze hanging over them, from
the heat acting on their wet clothes. Some one, I
forget who, had told me that many of them had been
in their places since seven o'clock, and as I looked at
them I felt full of pity, for I thought how dull and
drab their lives must be for them to crowd like this to
a lecture. There can be little else here to amuse them.

But my chairman began to speak, and I listened
with strained attention, for, indeed, I had a difficulty
in gathering the purport of what he said. Presently
it dawned upon me, though, that he was telling them
how interested he was in the lecture that was to
come, because it was on the subject of the catching
of whales, and whale-oil was of so much importance
in his business of spinning. So far all was well, but
now he began to tell that audience, nearly all of whom

were employed in his mills, what whale-oil was used for, and how it was used. In fact, he delivered a lecture on the subject, which did not conclude until 8.25; and even then he only reluctantly made way for me. No doubt he knew his subject thoroughly, and as time did not matter, I felt much entertained.

It was quite a pleasant experience, take it all round, but I had another surprise the next morning. Coming down at eight, and entering the morning-room, I saw there in conversation with my host a man whom I should certainly have taken for the lowest kind of tramp, had I met him on the road. Eccentricities in dress, I hope, make no difference to me, poor clothes have been my own wear for many years, for while at sea I often patched my raiment, until, as Jack said, " you couldn't tell which was the standing part," and still I say that this man's bodily coverings were an offence to me. He hurt the eyes, he looked so dirty, so unkempt, so regardless of all the decencies, cleanliness among them. And he had on a pair of awful old boots, shapeless trotter cases, which were unlaced, and into which the ends of his ragged trousers were half-tucked, as if he had shuffled into them on tumbling out of his lair, and had never thought of them since.

Seeing me come in, my host gave me a cheery good morning, and waving a hand towards the nondescript, said:

" My brother Ben. He's my manager down at th' mills."

Brother Ben muttered something I could not understand, finished his colloquy with his brother, and went away, not being asked to stay to breakfast. I have since heard that the two brothers possessed very little short of a quarter of a million of money, and I have often wondered what they did with it, or what good it was to them, or anybody else. I saw no young people about the house, so I assume that there were no children. But I don't know. A lady who was my hostess in a village near Bradford showed me a house and mill, and told me that the owner had been a mill-hand, was now worth (as we say) nearly half a million, and had three sons and two daughters, all of whom he made work in the mill for wages. They wore the usual mill-hand's dress, with clogs, and lived in the basement of the fine house, as they had always been accustomed to do, never spending or giving a penny towards the gracious, gentle things of life. My host was much better than that, but I don't think he had any children.

Perhaps the most extraordinary experience I have ever had with a chairman was at Christmastide a few years ago. I am very anxious to give no clue to either the name of the gentleman nor the place, for I would be deeply grieved to give him a moment's pain, recognising as I do how whole-souled and heartily he gave himself and his means for what he considered the highest interests of his fellow men and women. So I will only say that in that period of rest which lecturers usually enjoy between the middle of December and the middle of January, I received a letter, asking me what my fee would be to deliver a lecture at a place about 450 miles distant, on a night shortly after Christmas, beginning about 10 p.m. I had worked very hard that season, and did not want to go at all, but, of course, I could not send a blunt refusal. But I said that I was tired, it was my only period for rest, and that if I came I should want twenty guineas for my lecture, and first-class return fare. And I dismissed the matter from my mind with the posting of my reply, for I never dreamed that such terms would be considered for a moment.

My surprise, then, may be faintly imagined when I received a telegram the next day, "Please come on date, specified terms agreed." There was now nothing to do but go, and go I did. On arrival at the place it was evident at once that I was only one item in a long programme, and my chairman was, at tremendous expense to his mental and physical tissue, keeping the whole thing going. It was 10.45 p.m. before my turn began, and it lasted exactly half an hour. For the mixed audience was almost worn out, and many of them were over-fed as well. I afterwards heard that the efforts to amuse them had been carried on continuously from 8 p.m., the only stipulation being that none of them should leave before midnight. I make no comment whatever on the wisdom or otherwise of this stupendous altruistic effort; I can only hint at it, as I am doing; but think of it for a moment, four hours of miscellaneous entertainment, varied by eating and drinking tea, coffee and mineral waters! I have seldom seen a man more weary than the host was—poor fellow, he had lavished himself for what he felt was a good cause, and as for the money—that was a mere detail, for he was a millionaire. It is only now that I remember that I have not once alluded to his efforts as a chairman. Well, he was as near my ideal as can be, but such was the condition of the audience that, in spite of his lucid little introduction, I am firmly convinced that the great majority of them had not the least idea what to expect of me, did not in the least know whether I was a conjurer or a vocalist or a politician. And, as somebody said, it didn't matter, anyhow, his great end was achieved if he kept the people off the streets on that particular night, and if his lavish expenditure in order to instruct as well as amuse them seemed wasteful—well, it hardly mattered.

I will close these chairman reminiscences on a high note, one of the pleasantest recollections of my life, as well as one of the greatest privileges I ever enjoyed. In the summer of 1899 I was privileged to act as special correspondent for a London newspaper on board H.M.S. *Mars* during the summer manœuvres, and I spent then the jolliest time of my life. Towards the close of the manœuvres, however, things got a bit tedious, and during some golden days we lay (the hostile fleet, that is) somewhere off the Biscayan coast on a sleeping sea, awaiting some orders or some development that never came. In order that the men should not feel any lack of interest, much was done to amuse them, or to help them amuse themselves in the way of athletic sports, etc., and one morning Captain May asked me whether I would oblige him by giving the crew a lecture.

Now I had never lectured before without my slides, and I need not say how difficult such a task appeared to me, but I had not got them with me, and I could not refuse a request so kindly made; so I at once agreed, and was very graciously thanked. I may say that I was assured that if I had brought my slides with me, the absence of the lantern would have been no hindrance, for one would have been invented and fixed up somehow. And I am perfectly sure from what I know of the naval man that this feat would have been performed. However, I did not tax their ingenuity so far, and with the customary promptitude the lecture was fixed to come off that same evening.

Coming on deck after dinner, I was surprised to see in the middle of the broad quarter-deck a high platform rigged and draped with bunting, backed by the Union Jack. Right across the front of it chairs were placed for the officers, and behind them, stretching far away to the rear, rows and rows of mess benches neatly arrayed. A brief command, a short bugle call, and with the muffled thunder of hundreds of bare feet, my audience assembled, took their seats, and lit their tobacco. Amidst perfect silence Captain May mounted the platform, and introduced me in a brief speech which filled me with the deepest glow of pride and humble gratitude I have ever felt. Of course, I cannot reproduce it, but every syllable is indelibly printed on my heart, the more because that good friend and brave man passed away not very long after.

Then, amidst a deep thunder of applause, I mounted the platform. But for at least a minute I was unable to speak. The magnificence of the whole scene overwhelmed me. I looked down upon nearly 800 young men, the fine flower of our race, whose shrewd, strong faces looked keenly expectant, but all kindly towards me. I looked around at the mighty ship in all her beauty of strength and cleanliness, upon her seven gigantic sisters lying motionless in their exact stations near, at the soft splendours of the evening sky, and silken, many-coloured sea, and I felt truly that, although such a moment comes to a man but once in his lifetime, he cannot then appreciate all its wonders.

I did not attempt to lecture. I just fell back upon the well-known vernacular, and talked pure sailor, giving them all the yarns in my budget that were appropriate. And the time allotted me—an hour and a half—sped like a dream, punctuated by laughter and applause as generous and as full as only the handy man can give. And as soon as I had finished uprose the stately figure of the commander, giving in trumpet tones the formula to which I have so often listened in the public schools:

" Three cheers for Mr. Bullen ! "

I cannot say any more, except that the thunder of those cheers will echo in my ears until my dying day. They had hardly died away when my audience disappeared, mess benches and all, and the disciplined routine of the great ship resumed its course. The sequel, however, remains to be told, for it gives a keen insight to the tone of the navy man for his joke. As was my practice, I went on the navigating bridge next morning to glance at the signal log and greet the watch-keeper. The chief yeoman of signals, always a very able man, saluted me, and asked casually:

" Do you happen to know the ship's steward, sir ? "

" No, Flags," I replied, " I can't say I do. I know him by sight, but that's all."

" Ah, well," Flags rejoined, " he's a funny man, but a great chum o' mine. Last night, as we was a-goin' down from the lecture, he says to me, ' Flags, from 'enceforth I regard you as a perfectly truthful man.' I may as well say, sir, that I've 'itherto 'ad the reputation of bein' the biggest liar in the fleet."

And it was not until some time afterwards that I fully appreciated the somewhat oblique compliment.

CHAPTER XIII

LANTERNISTS

CHAPTER XIII

LANTERNISTS

NOW while it is perfectly true that I have never given my lanternist any trouble, and that all my slides are perfectly simple, and that I never have any of them repeated, I do not for one moment suggest that this is the reason why I have been so very fortunate in my experiences of lantern operators. Only on the rarest of occasions have I had any trouble, for which I am, I hope, duly grateful, for of all the disconcerting things that can occur to a lecturer, I think anything happening to his pictures through the incompetence of the lanternist is about the worst. True, I have always had much sympathy with my operators, looking upon them as very able men, who do a lot of hard work for a very small fee, and whenever a picture has been put on wrong, I have always, in asking the operator to change it, told the audience that the mishap was my own fault, except on one occasion, which you shall hear about.

I was to lecture in the Town Hall of a large town in the North of England, and my most charming and agreeable host was chairman. Just before we left the house for the hall he said to me gaily:

"We've got you a splendid lanternist. The last one wasn't a success, but this new one is super-excellent, I am told, and I am sure you'll find him so."

I replied nonchalantly, for I was not accustomed to have any trouble, and didn't see why I should begin now. So on interviewing the much-extolled lanternist I merely showed him which end of the box to begin, told him that the slides were all upside down and faces forward, and arranged the signal— all as usual. Then I thought no more about the matter, but at the appointed time faced a very large and enthusiastic audience, and after the chairman's brief introduction plunged into my subject. In time-honoured phrase, all went well until the fourth slide, which should have been about the twentieth, and was, besides, upside down. In a subdued tone I asked the lanternist to give me the next slide, hoping that this inopportune appearance was just an accident, probably an oversight of my own. Alas! no, the next slide was from another part of the box, and was, moreover, on its side. Begging the audience to bear with me a moment, I leapt off the platform, and ran to the lantern—to find the lanternist stupid with drink, and my slides mixed up in most gruesome fashion.

The sweat poured off me as I hurriedly replaced them in order, then begging the operator to put them in just as I had left them, I regained the stage, and was greeted with a hearty round of applause. I picked up the thread of my discourse at once, and four slides succeeded each other properly. Then chaos came again. Again I asked the audience to excuse me, again I visited the lanternist. I found the slides all jumbled up as before, and to add to my trouble, when I asked indignantly what he was doing, he replied sturdily that he was putting them in the carrier just as I gave them into his hands.

Well, that was a lecture, to be sure. Fortunately I did not lose my temper or my head, and the audience rose to the occasion, treating the whole business as a huge joke. Five times did I go down to that lantern, and rearrange those slides, and always after the first one or two placed correctly, the jumble would begin again. At last, with the audience almost in hysterics, I gave up all hope of getting anything shown that I wanted, and treated the rest of the lecture in a go-as-you-please fashion, making as many jokes as I could, until I found that the used pictures began to appear again, and, of course, that meant a sort of circular arrangement which would not end. So, finding that the time was up, I appealed to the man in charge of the lights to turn them up, and, disregarding the lanternist altogether, wound up with the audience rocking and shouting with laughter.

The chairman was as bad as the rest, so there were no votes of thanks, and, still laughing, the crowd dispersed. Feeling utterly done up and wet through with sweat, I made my way to the anteroom, where I was received with great gusto by the committee, the chairman especially, who said:

" Well, Mr. Bullen, we have never had a lecture before that we have enjoyed so much. I have laughed until I am sore all over. And yet it didn't seem to be a funny subject."

" I congratulate you," I replied, " but as far as I am concerned it would take a very few more of such lectures to be the death of me. I haven't a dry thread on me, and I feel as if I had been fighting for my life. I can only hope that when the next lecturer comes you will endeavour to see that the lanternist is sober. It is not at all just to the lecturer to have such a burden thrown upon him as I have supported this evening."

It is hardly credible, but, nevertheless, a curious tribute to my ability in hiding the lanternist's delinquencies, that all of them disclaimed any idea that there had been anything wrong with the lanternist, nor did a sudden searching aroma of whisky as that individual brought my slides in enlighten them. Of course he had left the last slide in the carrier, but that was only to be expected. What I did not expect was a sudden coolness on the part of the committee towards me after my statement, and I was never invited to that society again.

An extraordinary thing befell me once at St. George's Hall, London, on a Sunday afternoon, showing how a little carelessness on the part of an experienced man may cause much trouble. Those lectures were very well paid, well patronised, and limited to an hour, which allowed of no time being cut to waste. So I went ahead at my best, and was three-parts through my address when the light went out. Having had similar things happen to me before, I went on talking, thinking that a picture would soon reappear, but the darkness remained, so I presently stopped my address and asked the lanternist how long it would be before the next picture came on.

"There's no more gas!" he replied in hollow tones.

I will not repeat what I said when the lights were turned up, but it was in the nature of condolence with the audience, and indignation that for the sake of sixpennyworth of gas the lecture should have been spoiled. For that was what it amounted to. The lanternist had brought a partially emptied cylinder with him, the gauge of which indicated barely enough gas for an hour's work. A little waste for practice reduced that, so that three-quarters of an hour finished it, and we all had the mortification of being deprived of the sight of a dozen pictures, and of feeling that we had been defrauded by an unfinished lecture.

What would otherwise have been a very awkward business was put right by the promptitude and ability of a friend of mine, Mr. Charles Hoddle, who was among the audience, being my host for the night, and having motored me over. It was at a chapel, and after the usual preliminaries the lights were turned down, and—the first picture did not appear. In answer to a confused murmur from the gallery where the lantern was, I made some cheerful joking remark to the audience, and went on with the lecture. Three times I stopped and ventured an enquiry if the picture would appear now, and at last, feeling that if my patience wasn't exhausted, that of the audience was, I said :

" I wish you would let me know whether we are going to have any pictures or not, because, if not, we'll have the lights turned up."

A voice, with tears in it, feebly exclaimed in the gloom :

" I'm very sorry, sir, I can't get it to go anyhow. I've tried my very best, but I——"

A great roar of laughter extinguished his voice, and I was just about to ask my friend Hoddle if he could help us, when I saw him stealing away from his seat in the gloom. In less than three minutes the picture appeared, and there was no further trouble. Mr. Hoddle did tell me what the trouble was, but I have forgotten, and it doesn't matter, anyhow. But I was never more grateful for the presence and help of a man with presence of mind and who knew the business thoroughly.

What might have been a terrific disaster occasioned by the inexperience of a lanternist was only just averted by a hair's-breadth at one of my lectures in Sydney, N.S.W. It was at the Lyceum Theatre, in Pitt Street, a fine house, but very badly off for exits. In fact, the whole of the great gallery, by far the largest part of the house, emptied through the one door down a steep flight of steps into the very busy but narrow thoroughfare of Pitt Street. It was an electric lantern, a form of lighting for this purpose that I detest unless there are certain arrangements made for keeping the slides cool. This is easily done, as witness the safe and easy handling of cinematograph films, which used to be highly inflammable, and yet very rarely ignited, as they certainly would have done with an unadapted electric lantern.

It was the opening night of my season in Sydney, and the lanternist was engaged from one of the best houses in the place, so that I had a right to expect the best manipulation. Especially when the price paid was considered. As soon as I began my lecture however, I saw that something was wrong. As each slide came on it cracked, peeled, and was destroyed, the sight of the process going on on the screen being a most disquieting one for me. Still, I did not see what I could do without alarming the audience and spoiling the show, so I saw six or seven slides burn up one after another. Then I was just about to protest in vigorous language against such wholesale destruction as I had never seen before, when I noticed that the lanternist was in dire trouble. Dense smoke was beginning to rise from the lantern, and even as I looked the smoke burst into flame. People rose in their seats, and looked with great anxiety towards the lantern and the door. There was a general uneasy stir when the electrician, bless him, turned the lights up, and I, raising my voice, said:

" Don't mind the lanternist, friends, he's in a bit of trouble. It's all right, if you'll just sit quietly, and take no notice of him. I'll go on with the lecture, we can manage for a while without the pictures." And so we did ; in fact we had to do without them pretty much altogether for the rest of the evening, for that lantern was fairly used up. But I am thankful to say that nothing worse occurred, and the lecture closed in peace. After it was over, however, I told my agent that something must be done about that lantern. I would not face the possibility of another mishap of the same kind for all the expected receipts of the tour. Besides, I could not afford to lose the slides, as I only had one set of duplicates, and I carried no negatives.

So that matter was attended to, and all was well, as I fondly thought. But next night, when I arrived at the theatre, the dismissed lanternist was there, raising no end of a bobbery and threatening everybody concerned with all sorts of dire revenge if he were not reinstated. He had been a lanternist for so many years, and no one had ever found any fault with him before, and so on, and so on. Finally he worked himself up into a mad rage, and we were obliged to send for the police to remove him. On their appearance he cooled down at once, and we saw that it was only bluff on his part. Still, a watchful eye was kept upon him, and we were not further molested. Neither was there any more trouble with the lantern.

Away back at the beginning of my lecturing experiences, before I had thought of lecturing as a source of income, I had conceived the idea of giving a lecture at our little hall, the converted cowshed at Peckham, which the irreverent called Troy Town Cathedral. It was a great effort in which all our little band took part, and we proposed to have a collection, which might, or more probably would not, pay for the gas. A neighbouring chapel very graciously lent us a lantern, a magnificent tri-unial, and our genial little chimney-sweep superintendent assured us that he was a perfect lanternist. Ascertaining that twelve feet of gas would be ample for a two hours' show, I went to Brins', in Horseferry Road, purchased a cylinder of that size, and with great pains conveyed it to the hall. We hired a blind organist who was a street musician but had a wonderful repertoire of sacred music and a very nice organ flutina, to be our orchestra, and issued our invitations.

The honorary lanternist and his friends were well on time, and got all the gear fixed up, so that when I arrived all was ready for the pictures. And the audience turned up in very satisfactory numbers. So far everything was splendid, and I commenced my address with great confidence, getting everybody's attention from the commencement. But at the third slide I noticed that the light was so poor that the outlines of the picture could not be seen, and the following colloquy between the lanternist and myself ensued :

"Can't you give us a little better light, Tommy ? "

"I can't, bruvver. I've tried all manner of ways, an' I can't get it no better. I don't know what can be the matter wi' it."

"Well, if the pictures can't be seen, I can't go on," I argued. "It's no use me attempting to explain without the pictures."

There was a hideous pause, which was improved by the organist softly improvising, until suddenly the lanternist cried, with a despairing note in his voice :

"There's no more gas, that's what's the matter. I thought there was some'ink wrong."

"But twelve feet of gas ought to last two hours," I protested.

"I don't know anyfink about that, I only know there ain't no more 'ere. An' that's all there is about it."

Voice from the audience : "Go on with the yarn, governor, never mind the pictures. They'll do another time."

After explaining my difficulty at some length I did try and " go on with the yarn "; but it was a poor attempt, for I had looked to the pictures as a series of notes, in fact I had entirely relied upon them, and I had not had sufficient experience to teach me how to do without them. So I am afraid the lecture was a very poor thing indeed—and if the collection was anything to go by, it was so—for the total amount realised was one shilling and fourpence halfpenny.

As soon as the audience had gone an enquiry was held among ourselves as to why the gas had given out. Apparently it still remained a mystery, or the blame was put upon Brins Oxygen Company. But I knew full well, and so did several of the others, I am sure, that the gas had all been used in practising, owing to the inexperience of our lanternist. So effective steps were taken to secure an operator of skill and experience for our next attempt, and the trouble never occurred again.

I think when the few examples of incompetence that I have given are remembered, and that they are all that I have had experience of during a lecture period of sixteen or seventeen years, the conclusion must be arrived at that my encomium upon lanternists is fully justified, and that I have solid foundation for offering them my gratitude. But I must add one more instance of trouble, not at all through incompetence, but incredible folly, which occurred to me some years ago in a large northern town. The secretary of the society for which I was to lecture met me upon arrival at the station, and accompanied me to the hotel where he had engaged a room for me, as hospitality had not been offered. When he had seen me comfortably installed he left me, but just as he was going he asked me for my slides, telling me that he had to pass the hall on his way home, and he would leave them there. Now I had never hitherto been parted from my slides like that, and did not at all see the necessity, but a foolish dislike to appear distrustful of him overcame my reluctance, and I allowed him to take them away. I warned him, however, that they were all in order for use, and that he was to tell the operator so, as well as that when I came I would myself explain which end of the box I wished him to take first. It was also arranged that the secretary should call for me and conduct me to the hall shortly before eight.

In due time he arrived, and we set off gaily together, both in high spirits, for it was a fine evening. I was feeling particularly fit, and we both anticipated a good house. Arriving at the hall at five minutes to eight, I went straight to the lantern, where I found two men, one of whom greeted me cheerfully with:

" Good evening, sir. We've looked through your slides, and we've arranged them all right for you!"

I felt as if a lump of ice had suddenly been laid upon my spine. In fact I could hardly speak for a moment, but when I could, I grasped the first half-dozen of the slides, exclaiming :

" You've surely never dared to alter the order of my slides ! "

But they had. A glance was sufficient to show me that these two men, acting under Heaven knows what impulse, had deliberately disarranged my slides. I am usually proof against a sudden shock. But it was eight o'clock, and the lecture due to begin, so I will admit that I was upset. My hand shook so that I could not hold the slides, and I dropped a number of them, breaking six. Then despairingly I lumped them all into the box again, and bore them off to the anteroom, where I told the secretary that he must put the lecture off for a quarter of an hour, and that I would explain to the audience why they had been compelled to wait.

But I was now cooler, and I soon had the slides re-arranged ; while I recognised that I should do myself no good, and might, with two people like that in charge of my slides, be subjected to a bad break-down. So I went on as usual, apologised for the delay, and had no more trouble. After the lecture was over, however, I had a heart-to-heart talk with the secretary, which was quite inconclusive, since neither he nor I could form the faintest idea why the outrage had been committed. Nor have I ever learned, for I could not get speech of the perpetrators. I strongly suspect, though, that it was nothing more than careless curiosity at first, and then, the slides not being numbered and many of them not even spotted, the inquisitive ones could not put them right again. The childish yarn about arranging the slides for me was uttered on the spur of the moment, perhaps as a sort of impromptu explanation. However, I suppose it is hardly necessary to say that never again have I trusted anybody else with my slides until they were to be used.

CHAPTER XIV

AUDIENCES

O

CHAPTER XIV

AUDIENCES

I HAVE often been asked which I consider my best audiences. It is not an easy question to answer, for people vary so in different parts of the same county even. But I have no hesitation in saying that the northern folk, right away to Scotland, are almost uniformly good and quick. And as far as my experience goes, though it may be true (not in my experience) that the Scots joke with difficulty, I have never known any audience quicker or keener to note every point, or more generous with their applause than I have found in Scotland. Of course, in common with every lecturer, I suppose, no matter how long or varied his experience, I have affectionate recollections of certain audiences. The thought of them is very cheering to me in my retirement. I think of the sea of upturned faces now hanging on every syllable, now sending up peal after peal of laughter, and withal by their intense sympathy with me, urging me on to give them better words than I had ever known before that I possessed.

For I learned many years ago the prime secret of the successful—I was going to say orator, but the term is a bit fly-blown to me : it means stilted high-falutin rubbish, meaningless, and leaving any audience cold— lecturer. It is to get yourself on conversational terms with your hearers. This I do not think is possible with obviously prepared speech, and I am sure is impossible to the man who reads his address. The latter course is no doubt necessary at the Universities before a crowd of students with notebooks, seeking learning, and entirely unenthusiastic, but for a popular lecturer it is fatal. Shall I ever forget the look of woe with which I was greeted by a secretary at a big hall near London. To my earnest enquiry as to what was wrong he returned the astounding answer that the committee looked upon me as their only hope. If I gave them as good a lecture as I had given them on a previous occasion the society might survive, but if not it must perish. I wanted to know more, naturally, and the secretary then told me that with the laudable idea of giving their society the best talent obtainable they had engaged at a fee of twenty-five guineas an exceedingly big pot and eminent authority upon a certain subject.

He duly arrived, and appeared before a full house with a sheaf of manuscript, no pictures, a feeble, mumbling voice, and very bad eyesight. He could not decipher his notes, he was in trouble with his glasses, and he could not make himself intelligible. Before he had been on the platform fifteen minutes the hall was empty, and the chairman was compelled to suggest to him that he might as well retire. Within the week half the subscribers had indignantly resigned, and I was now expected to save the remnant, if not to win back some of the seceders. I think I should have been more than human if I had not asked that secretary whether he thought it quite fair to pay one man twenty-five guineas to destroy the society, and another ten guineas to rehabilitate it, but the question was not quite fair, since he was but the mouthpiece of the committee. Still, that question does arise occasionally, and will do so until societies learn that enormous fees to big pots do not always mean general satisfaction and increase of membership.

This recollection brings another in its train, as usual—this time a very delightful one for me. In the early days I went to a celebrated lecture society in London to lecture, and the secretary in conversation in the anteroom before the lecture told me, rather pompously I thought:

"We consider ourselves the best lecture audience in London. And our people will not stay and listen to what they do not care for. So if you find your audience melting away, don't be discouraged; it may only mean that your subject does not interest them, not any reflection on your ability as a lecturer."

I thanked him for his caution, but added that I thought I could have done without it. However, I would do my best, as usual. But I was piqued, and I believe I did strive to capture that audience. Anyhow I did get them, and the result remains with me always. For they took me to their collective heart, and together we romped through two hours of delight, at least so the clock said, but when I came off the platform I could not realise that I had been talking more than half an hour. Malapropos to the last, that secretary said to me:

"I don't think I've ever laughed so much in my life, Mr. Bullen, though, for the life of me, I don't know what I've been laughing about."

As if it mattered! The great fact was that even he, in whom a sense of humour was absent from his mental equipment, had laughed even unto physical disablement. Yes, that was a very pleasant evening, of a good savour even now.

I have told in another place of the great evening of my life in the Town Hall of Birmingham, and I am thereby precluded from adding very much on that head. I must add, however, that then, as never before, did I *realise* the utter blessedness of being in complete sympathy with a great company of one's fellow-mortals, of being able to talk with them as one of themselves, fearlessly, without any reserves or sense of weakness, conscious only of simple truth-telling, and your fellow's acceptance thereof. That supreme joy had been mine before, but unconsciously —that night in Birmingham was my first realisation of the great fact. Many and many a time when I used to preach in the open air, I have been enabled to forget overdue rent, shabby children, hardly sufficient food and bullying seniors in the office, in the pure joy of swaying a multitude of my fellow men and women, and taking them with me for a while into a rarer and purer atmosphere, where the sordid, irritating things of earth were forgotten in the better world of truth and justice.

It may seem invidious of me to single out certain occasions from the great multitude of happy lecturing hours that have been mine, but it is not so meant. I cannot help the fact that these occasions have impressed themselves indelibly upon my mind. Briarfield, Burnley! I do not often permit myself the luxury of mentioning the name of any place or person, but here I break what has become a rule with me most gratefully.

This was a strong centre of the noble St. John Ambulance Association, and my first experience connected with it was the hearty yet diffident welcome of the stationmaster at the little station— who behaved as if he would be genial, but did not wish to intrude. We speedily became intimate, and he conducted me across some fields to the house of a gentleman, who entertained me royally. When, accompanied by my host, I made my appearance at the hall, I was immensely gratified to find it full of eager folks, a large proportion of them in Red Cross uniform for both sexes. This was the first time I had ever been brought into contact with a centre of the Association, and I was much impressed by the keenness and earnestness exhibited by everybody. It was not, however, until I mounted the platform,

and began my address, that I realised the exceeding
warmth of my reception, and the great sympathy
felt by those present for myself. This led me to
devote a few minutes to my own experiences in ambulance work on board ship, where native wit had to
supply the place of training, and extensive reading
also helped with medical knowledge.

Greater interest and enthusiasm could not possibly
have been manifested than by this audience at my
anecdotes, and I was repeatedly interrupted by
vociferous applause. Here I feel bound to interpolate a statement concerning a characteristic which,
though personal to myself, I feel cannot be singular, it
must be shared with many other public speakers, but
whoever has the faculty of which I speak, surely
must feel as grateful for it as I do. I allude to the
power of being able to devote one-half or one portion
of the mind to any other subject which may present
itself, while apparently wholly engaged in the subject
upon which the audience is being addressed. Kipling
hints at this faculty in one of the poetic chapter
headings in *Kim* :

"Something I owe to the soil that grew—
　　More to the life that fed—
　But most to Allah who gave me two
　　Separate sides to my head.

"I would go without shirts or shoes,
　　Friends, tobacco or bread
　Sooner than for an instant lose
　　Either side of my head."

I have often envied others the power of concentration, but, oh, the sheer joy in being able to carry on two mental operations at once. To be able to devote yourself most strenuously to the desires of the audience, while at the same time reaching out with another most prehensile section of mind into quite different regions, and bringing back treasures long forgotten or unsuspected to lavish upon those beloved hearers who are giving you one of the great joyous times of your life. What I am writing may seem extravagant, but it is honestly true and honestly felt. Between every member of some audiences and myself there seems to be a chord of sympathy, a mental connection, compelling the delivery not only of *my* best, but of matter, the very existence of which has until then been unsuspected by me.

And of all the occasions upon which I have felt and exercised that delightful faculty, that night at Briarfield stands easily first. And it was curious, too. For I was totally unfit to stand before them at all, physically. Among the many mysterious things connected with this fleshly habitation of mine is one that involves much pain and discomfort, and for which I can never account. On that day I had been very leisurely indeed. My journey from London had been most easy and pleasant. I had read a gentle book, I had enjoyed a good meal. And on arrival at my host's house there was no excitement, for host and hostess were unavoidably absent, and I rested in a charming room, in one of the easiest of chairs, until their return two hours later. Yet when I went up to dress, my legs and arms were covered with irregular painful swellings and purple spots, which made any movement and standing very painful to me.

The experience is in no way unusual to me, I have had it for years, and when it attacks me nothing is of any use but a recumbent position. I have gone a long and wearying journey to Scotland, and lectured in some distant suburb of Glasgow, and never felt it, and on an occasion like that of Briarfield I have been in agony throughout the lecture. Yet, and this does give me pleasure, none of my audience knew, nay, I was only subconscious of pain myself, it ran like a hot wire through my thoughts. And I have often wondered whether bodily pain like that has any effect upon the thought centres, as a stimulant, let us say ! It may be so, but I know that I should have been grateful to do without such a stimulus.

In this connection I recollect on one occasion having to lecture at Winchmore Hill, when, as the phrase goes, I was suffering from a severe attack of neuritis. At least I suppose that is what it was, a pain like an incandescent wire running from my shoulder down the inside of my right arm to my finger-tips, paralysing my hand, and refusing to be eased, no matter how my arm lay. I had a sling for my arm, but it was of little use, for I had to be con- tinually withdrawing the limb from it when the pain grew unbearable. However, I got assistance in dressing, and arrived at the hall, to find the secretary full of sympathy, but very doubtful from my contortions and grimaces whether the lecture would come off.

I endeavoured to reassure him, told him of that mysterious uplift we get when we face the audience, —my brother-lecturers will know what I mean—and think I succeeded in allaying the most severe of his apprehensions. At any rate the time came, and I did face the audience, who showed by their laughter and applause how much they appreciated the lecture. But when I came off the platform I was chalky white, and wet through with sweat, while the pain—— But, there, that doesn't matter. What did matter was that the audience was not disappointed. For that is the great thing to avoid. There are no valid excuses in the lecturing business. If you let an audience down once, you may wipe that place out of your expectations for the future. At least that is my belief.

But how hard it is on a lecturer. I remember once being engaged not for a lecture, but to deliver an address to the Seventh Day Schools Association, Severn Street, Birmingham. I gave a lecture the previous evening at Dudley Port, and was in fine trim, never better. But when I awoke in the morning I could not utter a sound, my voice had gone ! I had no trace of cold, soreness of the throat, or any feeling save that of good health, but I was as dumb as a fish. I went to the gentleman who had engaged me, and with the aid of some paper explained my difficulty, offering to write out an address and give it to him to read, since he was to be my chairman. Naturally he was staggered, could hardly believe me. Nay, I am sure that he did not quite believe me, for in the evening after he had read the address I had written—and, oh, didn't he read it badly !—he asked me to get up and say " just half a dozen words."

In vain I pointed out to him on paper that I was utterly incapable of making the slightest sound. He still pressed me, until at last I stood up and faced that audience, feeling like the champion fool of all the world, for I was dumb. I made a few signs, and then with burning face sat down. I felt then, and I feel still, that, grievous as my friend's disappointment was, he need not thus have humiliated me. I am sure, though, that he did not think he was so doing, it was only his desire that his friends should see for themselves that I could not speak to them, much as I must have wished to exercise that privilege.

One audience that I addressed in a large northern town did fairly puzzle me. The hall was full, and I was in good form, but those people never gave a sign that they even knew what I was saying. They sat stolidly looking at the screen, but never making a sound, and though none of them went away until the whole thing was over, they preserved the same uncanny silence all through. No ! let me be just.

They did once applaud, and for that I was, and shall always be, grateful to them. My chairman was a most amiable schoolmaster, head of an important school in the vicinity, and he exercised his function as chairman in the most praiseworthy way.

So far, so good, but from the commencement of my address I had noted with growing disfavour the behaviour of the young men who occupied the front row of seats. They were evidently out for a lark, and showed it plainly by conversing with one another, gradually becoming more and more audible, until there was a serious interference with the sound of my voice. I grew more and more disturbed, until at last I could endure it no longer, and suddenly ceased speaking. Of course they did so too, so after waiting about a minute in a profound silence, I said gravely:

"I have been waiting patiently for you young gentlemen to finish what must be a very important conversation, since you must needs pursue it in a place like this, where it disturbs me in the performance of my duty, and prevents people who wish to listen to me from hearing. But I think it is very strange that you should come here to talk when you could find so many better opportunities outside. If, however, you feel that you must talk here, I must appeal to the audience whether they want to hear you more than me, and I will abide by their decision."

A vigorous burst of applause followed, and I had no more trouble, but went on to the end of my lecture in perfect silence. After I had returned to the ante-room my chairman said, pompously:

" I think you were much too severe in your remarks about the behaviour of those young gentlemen."

" Do you ? " I retorted. " Well, all I have to say is that some audiences I have addressed would have had them ejected long before. Their behaviour was that of a pack of uneducated cads."

He said no more, and I afterwards learned that those young gentlemen were his prime scholars. Hence his defence of their conduct. On my way home with my hostess I expressed my astonishment at the strange apathy of my audience.

" Oh," she replied, " that is easily explained. I doubt if ten of them understood what you said. They were nearly all German Jews."

Which set me wondering in another direction, although it did satisfactorily explain the principal mystery.

I feel I cannot do better than close this chapter with an account of an audience I once addressed in the Scotland Road, Liverpool, whither I was sent by the Corporation Lectures Committee, who had engaged me to give a series of free lectures in the city. I was accompanied by my friend and host, Mr. Charles Birchall, who thus generously gave up his valuable evening to keep me company, for he had heard the lecture before. We got a bit of a shock on arriving at the fine hall, when we saw the class of people that were going in, and my good friend took the first opportunity afforded him in the anteroom of putting his watch, chain and money in a place of safety before taking his seat.

On the stroke of eight I mounted the platform, and faced an audience of I should say 1200, but such a congregation as I have never addressed before, and hope never to again. It was evident at once that most of them had come in there for shelter out of the bleak and bitter night, for they were nearly all in rags or at any rate very poorly clad. And they smelt. Poor things, they looked wolfish from hunger, scarred with brutality, and desperate with want. And I was to lecture to them upon Romance and Reality at Sea! My mind was made up in an instant. A lecture in any ordinary acceptation of the term would have been not only a farce, but a dire insult to these hapless people, and so I drew upon my great stock of reminiscences of Liverpool Docks when I was young, of the realities of sea-life, of things, in short, that they could understand and appreciate. I don't know whether I made them forget my evening dress, I forgot it myself, I know, but it is certain that I held them from the start, and was rewarded at the close of the lecture, which lasted nearly two hours, with vociferous applause.

When I rejoined my friend he was almost speech-less with amazement. Knowing Liverpool so much better than I did, he had wondered mightily what I could find to say to an audience like that, obviously hungry, wretchedly clad, and vicious-looking. And then he had seen them interested, and applauding heartily, forgetting their own very present troubles in my recital of what they felt to be truly my own sad experiences as an unwanted waif of the street, lurking about the docks of that great city. I have since heard that some of my successors did not fare so well as I did, and I am not at all surprised at that, I should be more inclined to wonder if it were not so, when I recall the antecedents and careers of the most of them.

In all my experience I never met with a really unjust or unkind audience but once, and that was in a large town of Scotland. Through some carelessness on the part of those in charge of the proceedings the galleries had been allowed to become the playground of a number of noisy, thoughtless children, who amused themselves during my lecture by running about and jumping over the benches, accompanying their antics by shrill cries. I stopped and protested, suggesting either that the youngsters should be kept quiet or removed. To my utter surprise my remarks were received with hisses. I promptly thanked the audience and retired, saying that since they preferred rather to listen to the racket overhead than what I had to say, that I had much pleasure in leaving them to that enjoyment.

CHAPTER XV

AUSTRALASIA

CHAPTER XV

AUSTRALASIA

AFTER my visit to the United States on lecturing business, I gladly embraced the opportunity to go to Australasia on a similar errand, although, in the latter case, the venture was entirely my own. I mean that I was not engaged by anyone. More than that. I had an agent whose agreement with me was that he should have a free hand in spending money on my behalf, but that of the net proceeds he should take two-fifths, leaving the remaining three-fifths to me. My only safeguard was that we should have weekly settlements, but as that was treated as non-existent, it didn't make any difference, and I had the pleasant knowledge that all through my tour I was working to maintain three people. That, however, is a mere detail.

As was to be expected, my audiences in Australasia were very much smaller than they had been in America, but I gladly note that what they lacked in numbers they made up in appreciation. Perhaps this was to be expected, as I found that I was well and favourably known by repute in the Antipodes, which was certainly not the case in America. And besides the handicap of my being an Englishman was absent. This, however, is not the pleasantest of my recollections of that tour. At the time of my visit the total contributions of the whole of Australasia towards the expense of the British Navy was only £240,000 a year, or much less than the cost of a scout. One of my lectures ("The Way they have in the Navy") was an attempt to show my hearers what the British Navy really was, and in it I spared no pains to convince my Southern hearers that their attitude towards the Navy was not only ridiculously penurious, but fraught with the greatest danger to themselves. I very well remember impressing upon them, whenever I got the opportunity, that the amount contributed by the British people for the Navy was about £1 per head, and that if the Australasian people would only tax themselves to the same extent they would in five years have such a Navy as would afford them the protection of which they were now destitute. Nor could they reasonably expect the British Navy, if the mother-country was in danger, to spare a single modern warship for the protection of the Antipodes, all of whose cities lay near the coast, and liable to destruction by a single foreign war vessel of modern design and armament.

What the Australasian Dominions have done since then is a matter of common knowledge; if not quite as much as I recommended, still gigantic strides have been made, and I am grateful to feel that what I had the opportunity of saying by tongue and pen aided local effort sufficiently to bring about such a desirable result. At the time of my visit the obsolete cruiser *Powerful* was the most up-to-date vessel in Australasian waters, and the flagship of the Admiral, Sir Wilmot Hawkes. Then there came into Sydney the Japanese training squadron, three small gunboats, each of which mounted a twelve-inch gun, and though about one-quarter of the size of the *Powerful*, with armament sufficient to have sunk a whole fleet of *Powerfuls* at her leisure.

The object-lesson could not have been better timed, and I hope I used it for all it was worth. I know, at any rate, that I was severely censured for plain speaking, but I felt and said that the welfare of such cities as Sydney, Melbourne, and Adelaide was far before any personal considerations. But I proved then that both Press and people only wanted the facts pointed out to them for them to act. They were not content simply to turn over in their sleep and mutter, " Oh, it will last our time." Not they. And the recent naval activity of the Southern Dominions is the result.

Apart from this patriotic matter, the reception that I met with everywhere was most encouraging. It is true that I often had the misfortune in the smaller towns of coming immediately after or before a theatrical company, which had either swept up all the "joy-money," or it, the cash, was awaiting the advent of the fun-makers. Also I had to compete with the cinematograph in the large cities, which had just arrived, and was scooping up all the money in sight. And beyond that I was surely unfortunate in my time. Just after my arrival in Auckland from Sydney, and on the very day that I was to give the first of four lectures in Her Majesty's Theatre, came the upheaving news of Mr. R. J. Seddons' death, which affected the whole community more than an earthquake would have done. But not in the same way that it affected me.

For when the news arrived the city went immediately into mourning, and I was perforce compelled to refrain from giving my lecture that night. This was a very serious matter for me, for the expenses of each day, heavier in Auckland than in any town I visited, were about £80. And I was faced with that loss, because it was certain that I could not regain that lost day, as the theatre was let again immediately. I did try to get the company owning the theatre to meet me by cutting the enormous rental of the theatre for that unused night in half, but they would not hear of it, the loss was mine, and I must bear it, they said cynically. But that was not the worst. So great was the shock to the community that all businesses like mine felt it for a long time, and the three lectures I was able to give in Auckland did little more than cover expenses.

The late Prime Minister of New Zealand had many sincere mourners, but none who showed their sorrow in a more practical manner than I did, even if the exhibition was quite involuntary.

Now the North Island of New Zealand is quite an earthly Paradise, and although it was mid-winter at the time of my visit, arum lilies were growing rankly in the ditches about Auckland. Yet at Gisborne, only about 100 miles south of Auckland, I felt bitterly cold on the platform, a thing that has never happened to me before nor since. So cold was it that the speculator who had engaged me for those two lectures, at a fee of £40, made a very severe loss, because hardly anybody came the second night. They would not sit in an unlined galvanized-iron building to be half frozen, no, not to hear the most eloquent speaker living, much less myself, and truly I could not blame them. It has, however, always been a mystery to me how it could be so cold in that genial part of the world.

Considerable mystery attaches to my visit to Nelson. As a trip it was delightful, giving me as it did the opportunity of verifying the existence of Pelorus Jack, the celebrated grey grampus which for some inscrutable cetacean reason meets and for a short time accompanies every steamer that enters or leaves Tasman Bay by the French Pass. Upon such a well-worn subject I am not going to expend space, but I must just notice one matter that is not touched upon

usually by any of those who have written about this
sociable whale. The *Pateena* was going a full sixteen knots, so her captain told me, yet " Jack " played
round her bows without any apparent effort, and
occasionally would put on a spurt that carried him
a ship's length ahead, when he would slow down,
and allow the ship to overtake him again, and resume
his favourite pastime of wallowing in the turbulent
water just abaft her stern. And when he left her
finally, which he did after about twenty minutes,
he shot off at right angles from her, and almost
immediately disappeared. I therefore cannot put
his top speed at any less than thirty knots an hour.

But from a financial point of view Nelson was
a dismal failure, and I do not see how from its popu-
lation it could well have been otherwise. It may
have been bad management, however ; of that I
know nothing. Still as my object was not a pleasant
holiday, I was glad to get back to Wellington again,
where I had an excellent reception, which partly
consoled me. This was the more noticeable, because
here again I lectured in the theatre, where I followed
an excellent opera company, under the management
of Henry Bracy, who were giving all Gilbert and
Sullivan's operas. Yet, despite this, I was very well
patronised.

My hopes were now centred upon Dunedin, for
I knew that practically everybody there knew me,
and I felt very hopeful that my reception would go

far to make up for what could only be classed as failure hitherto. I was to appear in the Garrison Hall, the largest auditorium in the city, and although it was not crowded it was well filled. One of my old Dunedin friends, a very prominent man of business and an expert accountant, at whose house I was a guest, congratulated me upon the audience, but when I told him the amount of the takings he was dumbfounded. Presently he said:

"My dear Bullen, you are being robbed. At the prices of the seats there should be fifty or sixty per cent more money in the house than that. Who have you attending to the front of the house ?"

I replied that I did not know. My agent was in Wellington, and the very reliable and honest fellow who was acting for me could only be in one place at a time. My friend explained to me how easy it would be for dishonest people to keep a great deal of money from the takings at the doors, and then offered to come the following night and count the house, a thing he had often done before. Afterwards we would compare one another's figures. We did so. I had £74, his count made £135! And now I could see how this thing must have been going on all the time, and I powerless to help it in any way. The best proof of the correctness of his counting was in the fact that on a return visit which I paid to Dunedin before leaving for home I gave a complimentary lecture for the benefit of a fund for helping stranded seamen. The house was about the same, but, after all expenses were paid, there was £110 net available for the fund.

These are details, however, which only show the difficulties under which a lecturer labours who has to put up with an inefficient agent or an inequitable agreement. The people were splendid. I enjoyed everything else in the country most thoroughly—the charming scenery, the delightful audiences, the home-like hotels, the thoroughly good newspapers. And the kindly hospitality of Messrs. Huddart Parker and the Union Steamship Co. and the N. Z. Government railways, which relieved me of all expenses of travel except for my agent and the advance man, was very welcome indeed. But for this and the kindness of the Steamship Company that gave me a free passage out and home, I am afraid that I should have had very little to show for my tour in cash, notwithstanding the fact that in Melbourne, in a hall which cost £4 a night, I grossed between five and six hundred pounds in six days. But I had no control over the expenditure, nor was any account ever shown me, and as for the weekly settlement, that was from the first a dead letter.

Afterwards I learned that I was supposed to come back over my tracks and revisit the cities I had given lectures in, supposed that is by those who knew me, wanted to hear me, and had been prevented.

There were also many large places in Australia such as Ballarat, Bendigo and Brisbane to which I did not go, why I do not know. And so, as I began to feel very disheartened at the poor personal results from such great sums as were taken, I looked forward eagerly to my winter lecture tour at home, where, if the financial returns were modest, they were sure, and I never had the slightest reason to suspect that anybody wished to wrong me of a penny. So just when, as I afterwards learned, I ought to have been beginning the most successful half of my tour, I caught my ship at Melbourne, and started for home, where I arrived after an absence of seven months.

Looking backward over that period of my lecture career, I can see how good it was, and how well I should have been rewarded but for my ignorance in making the agreement I did. I might, it is true, have had bigger audiences in many places, but I could not have been better received than I was. And that not merely by the rank and file, but by all those in power of whatever political cast they happened to be. This was all the more delightful to me because I did not make the slightest attempt to push myself forward, and the kindly reception I got from governors and ministers was spontaneously tendered. One day in Wellington, when I was taking a walk, I thought I would leave my card at Government House, and write my name in the visitors' book, which I had been led to believe was the correct thing to do. I had done so, and was strolling away down the carriage drive again, when a messenger came after me, and told me that the aide-de-camp wished I would return. Of course I complied, and was immediately taken into the aide's room, who said that Lord Plunkett had seen me going away, and wished to have a chat with me.

I was then taken into his Lordship's room, and had a very pleasant interview with him for about half an hour, during which he expressed surprise that I had not been to see him before. He laughed heartily when I told him that my native modesty forbade me to take any advantage which calling on the great ones might give me, but though I knew I was often a loser from this diffidence, I could not alter it. But I have never been able to push myself forward in this way, and there's an end of it.

There is another thing which causes me to look back upon my Australasian tour with complacency. The experience which I then gained came too late to be of any financial benefit to me, but I fondly believe that it has been of some use to others. I have been very glad to put my knowledge at the service of anyone asking for it to whom it was likely to be of use, and I do not think that any lecturer of standing has since been caught in such toils as I was. And that is well worth remembering, I think. But here, if it will be of any use, I would wish to add, for the benefit of any brother-lecturer going to the

Antipodes, never allow your agent a free hand in spending, and insist upon a daily settlement. This can easily be done if the agreed terms are half the gross takings, the agent to pay all outgoings, except the lecturer's personal expenses, out of his half. In my case I only had three-fifths of what was left, after *all* expenses were paid—I paid my own—and in too many cases there was nothing left for me at all. And I never had a settlement, that is with vouchers, duly presented and signed. So that I did not, nor do I now know what all those huge expenses were for.

Still, I cannot too emphatically repeat that this was nothing to do with the audiences, which were of the very best I ever lectured to, or with the welcome I received everywhere, which was the warmest conceivable.

CHAPTER XVI

SECRETARIES

CHAPTER XVI

SECRETARIES

FOR some time I have remained doubtful whether I would head one of my chapters Secretaries, for several reasons, which I will try to explain. In the first place my relations with these gentlemen have been almost uniformly pleasant, and that is a state of things which does not lend itself to picturesque writing. In the second place I am somewhat timid of being misunderstood, and as I know that secretaries are sensitive (and with justice), I do not want to say a word that can be misconstrued. But in common justice to a very estimable body of men (and some ladies) I feel that I ought not to issue these recollections without some extended reference to secretaries, and so having as I hope cleared the ground a little, I will take the plunge.

In all the vast body of unpaid work which is done by people in this country for the benefit of their fellows I do not think any is so onerous as that part which is involved in what are understood as a secretary's duties. He is usually a man who is very busy in some trade or profession, but takes up the job of being secretary of his literary society in a spirit of pure altruism. If, as is often the case, he be a young and inexperienced man, he will soon discover that so far from assisting him in any way with his work (and the duties are by no means light), his colleagues usually confine themselves to finding fault with him, and finding more work for him to do. The busier he is, and the idler they are, the more critical will they be, until he will find in very many instances that he is doing all the work and getting none of the credit.

And it is very often niggling, exasperating work. The selection of a list of lecturers, say, half a dozen, from the lavish number upon all subjects provided by our friend Christy, really devolves upon him, although there is nominally a committee. At any rate, if any lecturer chosen should fall short of the general expectations, be a failure, to put it bluntly, the secretary will please to bear the blame, whether he had anything to do with the choice or not. If a certain lecture is a great success, and everybody feels pleased, as sometimes happens, in the universal satisfaction it is quite easy to forget that it was the secretary's choice, pressed against the inertia of the committee. If, on the night of the lecture, there should chance to be some counter-attraction, impossible to foresee by any merely human secretary, what a fool he must have been not to have foreseen.

How well do we all know that woebegone look upon a secretary's face as he says, " I hope we shall have a good muster, but there are two or three things on to-night, and we draw a mixed audience here, so that I am afraid many of them will go elsewhere."

Happy secretary if he can then chuckle over the thought that all the tickets are sold, and consequently the financial success of the course is assured. Otherwise a wet night, or an uninteresting subject, may mean a big deficit in the funds, the takings being insufficient to pay the lecturer his fee, to say nothing of other expenses. And of course it is the secretary's fault, he must be fully prepared for that. It is only very seldom that a secretary is found strong enough to rule his committee with an iron hand, and insist that if he must take the blame for untoward happenings, he shall have the main voice in all arrangements. Unfortunately, such a secretary is apt to develop into a tyrant with whom it is hard to deal, although I gratefully admit that the character is very rare.

Again, it is upon the secretary always falls the thankless task of negotiating with the lecture agency, when a change of previously arranged dates has to be made. Such cases will occur, but no one outside of the profession can realise what an enormous amount of troublesome correspondence they entail. The severe training of the agency staff in some little measure enables them to compete with this with more or less ease, but the secretary, unless he be a born business man, often finds himself in an amazing entanglement, from which he feels it almost impossible ever to emerge with the least credit. That these matters are straightened out at all is generally due to the kindly and methodical assistance given by the agency, and it is most pleasant to record that this is, as a rule, unstintedly acknowledged.

It is of no use disguising the fact that the lecturers themselves do often give the secretary a bad quarter of an hour. I am not now thinking of those secretaries who seem to imagine that no one but themselves has any idea of time, dates or engagements. Who will worry with correspondence, both agency and lecturer, weeks ahead of an engagement, as if other people had nothing else to do but write and say, " Yes, I have your date noted, and if I live will be on hand as arranged." No, I am now thinking of the usual secretary, who, having got his agreement signed, goes calmly on his way, until the day of the lecture. He knows that he has done his part, knows that at eight there will be in all human probability an eager crowd of some eight hundred people or so to hear the lecturer, but, being human, he cannot help wishing that he had just a line from the lecturer to say that it is all right. Of course, if we were all perfect in every respect, he would not worry, but—you never can tell, and a halfpenny post card is so easily sent, and makes such an enormous difference to the peace of mind of a man who is doing a lot of gratuitous work, and does not deserve gratuitous worry as well.

Yet it does happen that the minute hand of the clock goes steadfastly on towards the XII which will denote that it is VIII o'clock, and not a sign is received from the lecturer. Then just as everybody is beginning to wonder what the secretary will do, the lecturer strolls in, and is calmly indignant to learn that there has been any anxiety about him. Forgetfulness may explain, though it cannot excuse, such behaviour. I have been guilty of forgetfulness myself, but I am glad to say that on these occasions I have always arrived long enough before the time for appearing to relieve the secretary of that gnawing worry that he must feel if he is fit for his job when nothing has been heard from the lecturer, and he does not appear until the clock has struck.

But there are deeper depths than these for the hapless secretary. There are the occasions when the lecturer does not write and does not appear ? To my shame and sorrow be it said I was once guilty of such a crime, and I can only plead for forgiveness on the following grounds. I was booked to lecture at Croydon on a certain date which fell on a Monday. Now on Friday I had travelled down to Altrincham, having accepted an invitation to stay there with a dear friend until Monday. Unhappily I caught a very severe cold going down, and on Sunday night was delirious, the condition lasting over Monday. In my lucid intervals I remembered my engagement, but, most strangely, thought it was for Tuesday, and when on Tuesday morning I awoke sane, though very weak, my first thought was a glad one—I should be able to keep my appointment after all. I turned up my lecture slip at breakfast-time for the secretary's address, in order to send him a wire, and then discovered that my engagement was for the previous night! I cannot sufficiently blame myself for not letting the agency know my whereabouts, for the outraged secretary had rung them up, and they could not find me, my wife having accompanied me to Altrincham.

The condition of that secretary's mind with that packed hall before him, and not only no lecturer, but no news of him, I can never get out of my mental vision, and I feel that it was such a fault as I could never meet by any sufficient apology. I could not help falling ill, and I was perfectly justified in visiting a friend, but nothing could excuse my failing to let my agents know of my whereabouts when away from home during the lecture season, except when keeping engagements made for me by them. To finish the story. I was treated with the utmost courtesy and forbearance. They made another appointment for me much later on in the season, but the audience neither forgot nor forgave, and when I did appear the hall was barely a quarter filled, which, of course, penalised the wrong people altogether.

Another occasion I must refer to. Since I cannot find any fault, any reasonable fault that is, with secretaries, it is only fitting that I should admit some of my own. I was engaged to lecture at Ilford on a certain evening at a Presbyterian Church. Carelessly glancing at the engagement slip, I did not notice with sufficient precision where the church was situated, but as I had for some years lived near Ilford I did not trouble about that. I knew, or thought I knew, where the place was. I lived in the country then, so I stayed at a hotel in London, and in good time dressed and caught my train from Fenchurch Street. I had hardly been in the train a minute before I realised that I had left my engagement slip in the hotel. It did not trouble me at all, for I felt sure of where to find the *Congregational* Church. Now, why or how the denomination got changed in my mind I cannot tell, but I know that until past nine o'clock I scoured Ilford, vastly grown and changed since I knew it, and could find no Congregational Church that was open or where there were any signs of a lecture.

So I was fain to return, beaten and horribly ashamed of myself, because I, being a Londoner, and withal well acquainted with that particular neighbourhood, had failed to find the place where I was to lecture. Also that I had been so careless as to leave my instructions in my room at the hotel. I found immediately upon my return what a stupid mistake I had made, and at once sat down to write the most complete apology I could compose. I offered no excuse for myself, indeed, I don't think I could frame a decent one, and I also offered to agree to any proposal that the secretary might make.

That gentleman replied very kindly and courteously, proposing that I should deduct all the expense the society had been put to from the amount of my fee, and fixing another date. I thankfully agreed, and I am glad to say that the audience on my second date was a bumper one. But the pastor, who was my chairman, did his duty by me as a faithful friend. He produced a MS., which he flourished before my eyes, saying that after his previous experience, when he had to rake in his memory for something to tell the congregation, so that they should not go away utterly disappointed, he had come prepared for any little forgetfulness on the part of Mr. Bullen. After a few more pleasantries of the sort, I stood up and confessed my offence, repeated my apologies, and then said that I did not know whether it was or was not an aggravation or a palliation of my offence that it should be the first time such a thing had happened to me in a lecturing experience of sixteen years, and a delivery of over a thousand lectures. I did not mention the Croydon affair, for I was then ill, and had I not been I should certainly have kept my engagement. And the rest was joy.

Three times in the course of my lecture career I have been approached by secretaries, all, as I well remember, paid officials, to ask if I would reduce my fee, *after* the lecture. The excuse in every case was the same: the low state of the society's funds. My answer was in all cases the same, i.e. had I been asked before the engagement whether I would under the circumstances lecture for a reduced fee, the opportunity of choice would have been afforded me. But I always went on to ask on what grounds of equity could I, a single individual earning my living, be expected to contribute several pounds to the funds of a society consisting of several hundred people. And the answer was always that my objections were perfectly just, and that had the secretary been able to exercise his own option, he would not have put such a request to me, but that, being a paid official, he had to do as he was told.

Now I would not for one moment attempt to dissuade any of my brethren or sisters of the lecture platform from *giving* their services in the cause of charity, when asked to do so beforehand. But I would strongly urge them always to insist upon their full fee being paid to them, and then making it, or part of it, a donation to the funds. For if a lecturer consents to give his services, he may be very sure that he will get a very poor audience, no one will think it is worth their while to work in order that his, the lecturer's, efforts in the cause of charity may be successful. In a word, what people get for nothing they do not value, which is an old but much ignored axiom.

In this connection I would like to mention an experience of my own in Scotland, although I may not give the names of the two places. It was in bitter winter weather, very snowy, when I arrived, and the town looked frost-bitten. But the hall where I was to lecture was a beautiful one, warm and comfortable, and the great library and reading-rooms attached were well filled. The secretary, a genial, jovial gentleman, bade me heartily welcome, and introduced me to several grave magnates as the members of his committee. As the clock struck we all filed on to the platform, and to my consternation there was just one more person in the audience than there was on the platform.

This might well have daunted the chairman, for the seating accommodation stretching blankly away before him was for 800. But it did not in the least that I could see. He took up his parable, and performed his duties with just the same air of ponderous gravity as he might have assumed in addressing an audience of thousands. And I could do no less than follow his good example, though I did feel glad when the lights went out, and enabled me to forget that great empty space. After the tedious formality of votes of thanks had been performed to the bitter end, I eagerly sought the secretary for an explanation. He told me that it was quite a frequent experience, because the lectures were well endowed and absolutely free, repeating the axiom which I have quoted above.

I unburdened myself to him, for he was exceedingly sympathetic, and said that while I didn't mind a small audience, there were limits, and I earnestly hoped that I might never have that night's experience again.

Vain hope. The following night I went to another large neighbouring town, the white weather still continuing, and again I faced an audience of fourteen, all told—no committee this time—and again a pleasant secretary told me the same disheartening tale. He, however, was more of a philosopher than my friend of the previous night, for he said that as long as our salaries were paid, and we did our best, the meagre attendance ought not to affect our happiness in any way. I agreed that it ought not, and yet —hang it all !—I couldn't help feeling somehow morally to blame. Utterly foolish, I know, but there it was.

It was some years before I visited those two places again, and when I did I had a vivid recollection of my previous experience. So that as soon as I met the secretary of the first place I said that I approached the lecture with considerable reluctance, feeling that it was like taking money under false pretences. He laughed cheerily and said :

" You'll be all right to-night. The hall is already full, and it wants a quarter of an hour yet to eight o'clock. And we shall be turning people away the whole fifteen minutes."

I stared at him amazed, and as soon as I got my breath demanded an explanation of this extraordinary phenomenon. Very quietly he assured me that the sole reason for it was that a charge of 2s. 6d. was now made for tickets for the whole course of eight lectures, with the gratifying result that the hall was now much too small to accommodate the crowds that besieged its doors every lecture night. And we shook hands over this patent endorsement of the theories we had both enunciated. Next day I went on to the other town, full of curiosity and eager hope that all would be well there too. So hopeful was I that the fact that the town was in the furious throes of a by-election did not trouble me at all. Yet we all know that if there is one thing more than another that can bring all a secretary's hopes and plans to the ground, it is to have a by-election clash with a lecture. It even affects the female part of his audience.

When, therefore, I met the secretary, and saw that his face wore its usual unperturbed expression, I ventured to say something in a commiserating tone about the by-election. He smiled gravely and replied :

" I don't think you'll find it make much difference to the meeting."

I did not like to ask him whether that would be because the attendance was so meagre, for I feared it would be, or might be personal, so I said nothing more upon the subject. But when the time arrived, and I made my way towards the hall, I was very much struck by the number and excitement of the people in the streets, who all seemed to be going my way. And when I reached the hall I was a bit excited myself to find the entrance, which was a long corridor, filled with loudly talking people, who did not in the least resemble a lecture audience. So much did this impress me that before I had got very far through the crowd I asked one of my neighbours why there was all this excitement about the lecture. He promptly informed me that *this* was a political meeting, and that the lecture hall was *next door !*

So I lost no time in changing my direction, finding, to my intense delight, that my audience was complete, and though sedate, evidently highly expectant. Every seat was occupied, and there were over a hundred standing. I afterwards learned that the reason for this change was the same as at the neighbouring town, the change from a perfectly free lecture to one for which a small charge was made. Still, I never before had such a gratifying experience as to find that the attraction of a political meeting next door was not sufficiently potent to attract my audience away from me. And I felt, I must admit, proportionately elated.

I think that by this time it must be sufficiently clear that my opening remarks about secretaries were quite justified, that I have little to say about them because I have found them so uniformly good. It is really the case. I do not in the least know what the agency's experience of them may be, but I must speak as I found them. Three secretaries I have known who were ladies, and they were perfect in courtesy and business-like habits. We had in two cases some little hilarity, owing to my addressing a lady as " M. Jones, Esq.," but then as I put it to them, if the word " Miss " is not put in brackets before the initial of a Christian name, no blame can be attached to a correspondent who assumes that the writer is of the male persuasion.

Let me close this chapter by assuring secretaries, one and all, that I carry into my retirement none but the pleasantest recollections of their uniform courtesy and kindness to me, often manifested under most trying circumstances. I would also like to add my whole-hearted admiration of the way in which these gentlemen (and ladies) perform their, for the most part gratuitous, and certainly onerous, duties.

CHAPTER XVII

DISCURSIONS

CHAPTER XVII

DISCURSIONS

SPEAKING generally, I have no doubt that it is true that an experienced traveller is far less liable to get into trouble on his journeys than a novice. But that any experience, no matter how great and varied, can render a traveller immune from the troubles of travel is a fond and vain superstition, only believed in by those who have had no experience. Take a recent experience of my own, for instance, and with it comfort, ye who have hitherto blamed your own inexperience for trouble into which you have fallen on some journeys. I am a Londoner, and I lived in London at the time of which I speak. I may say that although my experience of travelling in London and elsewhere was extensive and peculiar, I was handicapped by a great difficulty in breathing which made it hard for me to get about in this rapid age.

It chanced that I was due to lecture at Charterhouse one Saturday evening, and had, as usual, planned to return home after the lecture. It had been foggy the previous day, and the South-Western system, according to its wont in fog, had gone all to pieces, but twelve hours of perfectly clear weather had been experienced since, and I trusted therefore that my late afternoon train would be running as usual. But when I arrived at Waterloo I was met by the all too frequent experience of travellers whom a cruel fate condemns to use that most labyrinthine of stations, viz. an utter ignorance on the part of the officials as to when my train would start or which platform it would start from. Crowds of bewildered passengers hurried from one gate to another, badgering and exasperating the helpless officials with utterly futile questions, until, I suppose in desperation, a whole lot of them were embarked upon a train bound somewhere. How gladly they passed in through the barriers, had their tickets clipped and took their seats. And how wretched was their condition when, the train being full, an official arrived from somewhere, took down the direction board, and replaced it with a totally different one, resulting in the whole of them being turned out and cast adrift again.

But that such things happen continually at Waterloo I might endeavour to emphasise them, in order to be believed, but we all accept the South-Western as we do any other affliction which we are powerless to avoid, cease to wonder at its vagaries, and resign ourselves to them with what philosophy we may. I shall only, therefore, add that I did get a train to Godalming, starting only an hour late, but I learned that it was a train which should have started an hour earlier than the one I had intended to go by. However, I arrived at Charterhouse in time for a little dinner and my lecture, and was hospitably offered a bed by Mrs. Fletcher, as the running of the trains was so capricious. But I had said that I would return that night, and there was, very wisely, no 'phone at the school. However, it was arranged that the motor should run me down to the station, where, if I found the time-table to be still out of action, I was to 'phone home and return.

But when I arrived there I found the night beautifully clear, and an official emphatically assured me that the 9.33 to Waterloo would run on time, so I dismissed the car, and in due time, punctual to the minute, caught my train. In hallowed phrase all went well until we reached Woking, where a large number of passengers joined the train for Waterloo. But it did not leave, and to all questions the officials replied that they knew no more than their questioners the reason for the delay. Suddenly the fatal cry resounded from end to end of the train, " All change." That packed train-load of people crowded the platform again, and the train we had left was shunted into the middle line of rails, where it remained to tantalise us by its ineptitude.

In cold and misery and apprehension we all waited on that platform until at last a train came in which landed us at Waterloo at 11.45. The tube served me well, but I was nearly exhausted after changing at Piccadilly Circus and Leicester Square, and there I found the Highgate Tube in an awful muddle. Platform and trains were alike jammed with people, and the train men could not work. We were pulled out of the trouble by the energy of the driver, who came to the rescue of the guards, until at Mornington Crescent our load lightened a bit. Eventually I arrived at Highgate at 12.25, in one of the densest fogs of my recollection. All traffic was stopped, I was two miles from home, all uphill, and hardly able to stand from pain and racking cough. And it was bitterly cold. I battered at the door and rang the bell of the Archway Tavern, but it had only recently closed, and my summons was reasonably treated as that of some drunken wanderer.

I was very near collapse, and began to think of the immediate possibility of this being my end, for every breath I painfully drew was laden with death. Then a policeman hove in sight, to whom I addressed an appeal to get me in somewhere, weighted with half a crown. But he said there was nothing nearer than Finsbury Park, well over a mile away, except a doss-house, to which he dared not send me. And then he suddenly remembered having seen not far away a hansom cab with a poor old driver who had made practically nothing all the week. So he left me, and went in search of the cab, and in a very few minutes I had offered that poor old cabman half a sovereign to get me home. To say that we were both overjoyed is to put it very mildly. After seeing me safe inside, and the front let down, he started his old horse on a walk through the dense hedge of fog, but there was nothing in the way, and between us we found my home in half an hour. And when I sank upon a chair exhausted in my own room it was 2.20 a.m. But I was saved. I am thus prolix only to show how all my experience and local knowledge could not help me in these circumstances from having one of the very worst times of my life, and it was a wonder that I was not found dead upon the Highgate pavement.

A delightful recollection of mine is of an experience at the faithful city of Londonderry, an experience which I can afford to laugh at and enjoy now, but which at one time certainly began to look sinister. I arrived at the Great Northern Hotel in excellent time, for my lecture was not until eight, as usual, and my train was in about six. The secretary being very hard driven did not meet me, there was no need, for all was plain and straightforward. I had a chop, and while consuming it enquired of the waiter the way to the Y.M.C.A. Hall, where the lecture was given on my previous visit, but the way to which I did not remember because I had been taken there by the secretary. The waiter pointed to the old wall opposite to the hotel, showed me how to get to the top of it, and assured me that if I followed it round for about ten minutes I should arrive at my destination, for it was on the wall.

So I set out, not without some misgivings, for the night was very dark, and there was a high wind with driving rain. My breathing made the going in that exposed position very difficult, and I did not meet a single person of whom I could enquire, though I was certainly following my instructions. At last, after I had walked for twenty minutes, I felt sure I must be wrong, and looking over the wall into the street below, I spied a man, of whom I enquired if I was going right for the Y.M.C.A. Hall. He looked round him with that vacant air that in a citizen so annoys the strange enquirer of his way, and was about to direct me downhill or back again whence I had come. So I hastily said:

" All right, if you don't know, never mind; but don't you direct me back down that hill, for I won't go. If I do I can't climb it again."

" All right, sir," he replied cheerfully. " I was only getting my bearings. Ye'll go this way." And he pointed up a side street, giving me a mass of intricate instructions, during which I noticed that he was comfortably drunk. However, I had got half-way down the steps towards him by this time, and I felt disinclined to ascend, so I thanked him and followed the first part of his directions up the side street. It led me to an open space—a kind of market-place, I think, where I found two of those splendid fellows, the R.I.C., who speedily directed me right. But even then I made a mistake, for of two large buildings opposite each other I chose the one that was lit up, and into which many people were going. As I mounted the steps I was assailed by a host of ragged children, crying, " Taksinwiye, Taksinwiye," so loudly as almost to deafen me. I passed steadily on, saying, " I don't understand," although it was gradually borne in upon my consciousness that they meant, " Take us in with you."

And then I found that it was not the hall at all, and that a concert was about to commence ! So I went, dubiously enough, to the dark, unlighted building opposite, and entered the open door, to find it deserted. And the clock struck eight ! Utterly bewildered I stood in the flagged corridor and consulted my form of instructions, but here, at any rate, I could find no fault. Yet something was woefully wrong. As I stood wondering a young man came in, who, though a member, knew nothing about the lecture, and with that innate courtesy which is so pleasant a trait of Irish character, immediately devoted himself to my service. He bounded upstairs to the hall, to find it in darkness, and then offered to take me to the secretary's house, that being the only thing he could think of doing.

By this time I was resigned to the thought that I had come from London to the extreme north-west coast of Ireland to lecture, and by some fiendish complication had missed it, so I walked down the street by his side and said nothing. Suddenly a small boy, in a very smart scout uniform, rushed up to me out of the darkness, saluted and asked :

" Please, sir, are you Mr. Bullen ? "

" I am, my lad," I replied wearily, almost too much spent to wonder at this strange thing. Again he saluted and said :

" Please, sir, the lecture's in the Town Hall, and I've been sent to find you and show you the way there."

" All right," I answered. " Kindly hurry back and tell the Deputy-Lieutenant (my chairman) that I have been lost, but am now on my way, and will arrive shortly."

And it was so. The lecture was the first to be held in the magnificent new building which the good citizens of Derry have erected, but when I arrived at its noble portals and found that it was practically next door to the hotel whence I had issued three-quarters of an hour before I felt confused in my mind. Fortunately, a most enthusiastic scout-master had offered the services of his troop to act as stewards, and when the lecturer did not turn up at the appointed time they were delighted to go in search of him, with the result as described. And we started the lecture only twenty-five minutes late after all. The secretary had done his part; he had written to the agency to warn them of the change of hall, but their letter had missed me, he had also mentioned it at the hotel, but it was an Irish hotel, and that is enough said upon the subject.

Apropos of Irish hotels, I am pleasantly reminded of an experience at Cork. My dear old friend, Mr. Lane, wanted to put me up at Vernon Mount, but I had to leave Cork for Belfast by a train at something like 6 a.m., and so he took a room for me at the Station Hotel. Then he interviewed the boots or sub-deputy-boots, I should think, a wild kerne who looked as if he had never got over the shock of being born. To him Mr. Lane said, with tremendous mock severity :

" Now, look here, ye omadhaun, this gentleman *must* be called with a cup of tea at a quarter-past five to-morrow morning in order to catch his train at six. If you let him lose that train I'll kill ye as dead as meat. D'ye mind me now ? "

Trembling in every limb, and with his eyes fixed upon Mr. Lane's benevolent countenance till they seemed as if they would start from their sockets, the poor wretch repeated several times :

" Yis, sorr, yis, sorr ! "

Mr. Lane and I said farewell, and I turned in. Now I have always been able to wake at will, at least since I left the sea, and I have only to remember on going to bed at what hour I wish to rise and that time I wake. So I had no fear. And I awoke at five, rising and making a leisurely toilet. At 5.30, feeling that I should like that cup of tea very much, I opened my bedroom door to go in search of it, when at the first step I took in the dark corridor

I fell headlong over the prostrate form of the sub-deputy-boots, who was solidly asleep upon the mat at my door. He had nothing to say that was intelligible, but listened, as I thought, to my request for a cup of tea. Then he fled, and I saw him no more, but happily I had only to cross the platform to my train which had a breakfast car attached, so all was well.

Yet another Irish experience. I was staying with some very dear friends at a delightful little town on the County Down Railway, and on a certain evening was due in Belfast to lecture at eight o'clock. My friend and his wife accompanied me, and very jolly we were. Suddenly the train drew up at a large station, and I said cheerily, " Here we are, then."

" Oh, no," chirruped my host, looking out of the window. " This is Holywood. Next stop's Belfast."

So as I had not seen the name-board, and as my friend used that section of line twice nearly every day of his life, I did not bother, but resumed the pleasant conversation. After what I thought was a rather long wait, we began to move out of the station, *but in the wrong direction !* Upon my remarking the fact, my friend said airily :

" Oh, they're only shunting. They often do that at Holywood, to get the train on to its right platform at Belfast."

But the rate of the train accelerated until suddenly we rushed through Holywood, and my friend smote his knee forcibly, crying to his wife :

" That *was* Belfast, and this is the fast to Bangor !
We'll not stop till we get to Bangor ! "

My thoughts flew to that great audience in the
Grosvenor Hall awaiting me, but I realised that I
was in Ireland, where things have a way of adjusting
themselves, and nobody seems to mind. A great
deal of the personal element was to the fore during
the next hour, and eventually I turned up on the
platform only half an hour late, to be uproariously
welcomed by two thousand people, who took the
whole affair as a huge joke.

With hardly an exception a lecturer is treated
in this country with every kindness and consideration,
and if there are occasionally some thorns in his lot,
he has usually himself to blame. But, in spite of
Grish Chunder's saying that there are no exceptions
to no rules, I do believe orthodoxly that every rule
has its exception, and once in this country I had
the misfortune to meet with such an exception.
In accordance with my usual procedure I shall endeavour to veil the identity of the place, and I hope
to succeed, but I think any unbiased person will
agree with me that the treatment I experienced
was most cruel and inexcusable.

I came to this lecture from across the Irish Sea,
and put up at a town near, where there was a large
hotel, capable of accommodating several hundred
guests, but at the time of my visit quite empty.
The weather was very bad, for it was blowing a gale
of wind, with snow squalls, and I did not stir out of

doors until it was time for me to go to my lecture. Of course I dressed first, I mean I got into evening dress with a fine warm overcoat over all, and paying my bill, I took my baggage with me, because places such as the one I was going to had invariably put me up—it was the rule. I boarded the electric car, and in due time was dropped, apparently, in the open country, everything being hidden under a foot of snow. But the conductor directed me which way I should go, and after a painful pilgrimage of a quarter of an hour, during which I got wet to the knees, I found the buildings of which I was in search. Even then I could not find my way in for some time, and when at last I did, it was time for me to begin my lecture.

The gentleman who received me offered me dinner, but the audience was waiting, and I declined, except for a hot whisky and water, for my feet and legs were saturated with snow water. But I was buoyed up during the lecture with the thought of a comfortable meal and a warm bed awaiting me, so I hardly heeded the wretched state of my feet. When, then, the lecture was over, and more refreshment was offered me, I replied gaily that I would go to my room and change first, if they didn't mind. Then I was told that no provision had been made for me, and that I was expected to retrace my way through that wretched night to the hotel I had left several miles away. I was horror-struck. I protested that it was surely impossible that in an institution of that enormous size, where hundreds of people lived, room could not be found for one stranger on a night like that. But my interlocutor was obdurate, and I had to lug that great bag of mine back to the cross-roads through the snow, and there await the electric car.

I reached the hotel after eleven o'clock, pitifully cold, but not hungry. I was past that. And was shown at once to my room, where, for the first time in my life, I was unable to sleep in a fairly comfortable bedroom, on account of the cold. Indeed, after I had been in bed some time, I got up, and, walking briskly up and down, tried to restore my circulation. Yet I suffered no ill effects from the treatment I had received, except that I felt, and still feel, what I believe to be a righteous glow of indignation against the authorities of such a place who could treat any fellow-creature who was their guest in the way they treated me. But it was my first and last experience of the kind.

A delightful yet almost disconcerting experience befell me once in the early days of my lecturing, before I had learned not to be so lavish in *giving* my services, because of the harm I was doing those whose living it was to lecture. I was invited to give a lecture free to the members of the Pupil Teachers' Association at Toynbee Hall, and asked to choose my own subject. I accepted, and chose the subject of " How Poetry has helped Me." Now, being impressed by what I considered the educational importance of the occasion, I did what I have never done before or since—wrote out my lecture to the extent of twelve close-packed foolscap sheets. When I came to the time and place of meeting I was aghast to find that I was the only male person present, my audience consisting, with the exception of several High School mistresses, of blooming maidens between the ages of fifteen and twenty—some hundreds of them. My chairwoman was that excellent lady Mrs. Barnett, wife of the lamented Canon Barnett, then warden of Toynbee Hall.

Well, what with my unusual audience and the unusual experience of having a written lecture and no slides, I was rather ill at ease, the only time that I can ever recollect feeling so upon a public platform. After a few graceful words from Mrs. Barnett, I rose, amid gentle hand-clapping, and plunged into my subject, reading steadily down nearly to the bottom of the first page of my MS., and then a new thought struck me. I looked up from my MS. and went on, forgetting all about my written matter, until suddenly remembering it I was about to resume where I had left off, when I noticed that my time was up ! So I wound up with a few sentences, in which I alluded pathetically to my poor MS., and sat down amid really loud applause.

Then my chairwoman, during an interval of tea and cake, informed me that my audience would now entertain me with a selection of old English dances,

if I cared to witness them, and naturally I said I would
be delighted. So after signing a few dozen autograph
books, an arm-chair was placed upon the dais for me,
and there I lolled at my ease, like any Eastern Khalif,
watching those Houris threading the mazy con-
volutions of the dance. I have a keen sense of the
incongruous, and I confess that never in my life
have I felt it more strongly than then, for, in the
first place, dancing has never appealed to me, especially
ballet dancing, and in the next, I seemed to myself
to be more utterly out of place than I ever imagined
I could be. Yet I can have nothing but praise for
the kindness, courtesy, and assiduity of all present—
who could none of them have known how utterly
awkward I felt. Indeed I was glad when the evening
was over.

Only once more in my life have I had the same
feeling, and that was at the splendid Girls' School at
Cheltenham. My hostess, who was an enthusiastic
alumna of the school, told me that I must on no
account miss the wonderful sight of Miss Beale
reading prayers in the morning and the trooping
in of the 1000 scholars more or less. By some means
that I do not remember I was got into the school,
and given a seat upon a small dais close to a reading
desk, facing the great bare hall. At a given signal
the huge crowd of young ladies trooped in, filling
every available seat, and when they had all subsided,
Miss Beale, a short, stout lady in black, with a

dreadfully bruised face and a black eye, came in and stood at the desk.

She read the prayers and a chapter in a splendidly sonorous voice, during which the silence and attention was quite painful in its perfection. She ceased reading, and, turning sharply to me, whom to all appearance she had not noticed before, said, in a voice that rang deeply through that profound silence:

" You must go now."

Ah, me! was ever worm so crushed. My face and neck burned. I wonder my clothes didn't catch fire, as, muttering something unintelligible, but meant to be apologetic, I stumbled off the dais, and, pierced by those two thousand merry eyes, found my way out. Then the revulsion set in, and I felt hideously angry, because I felt sure I had been led into that false position for a joke, and that I had no business there at all. But I learned that the true reason was that the wonderful old lady had just sustained a bad fall from her tricycle. She had recovered with marvellous celerity, considering her age, but there could be no doubt that the occurrence had affected her temper, and who could wonder if it did? Still, I wished most sincerely that some other lightning-conductor might have been found than myself, or that one other man might have been there to lend me a little moral support. I felt just as if I had been caught in some prohibited meeting and was being led off to execution.

CHAPTER XVIII

DIVAGATIONS

CHAPTER XVIII

DIVAGATIONS

LECTURING, as I believe I have said before in these pages, is a most fascinating pursuit, though few who listen would imagine how it exhausts its votaries. And by this I do not mean those astonishing people of whom we are told that they come off the platform dripping with sweat, necessitating their being stripped, bathed, and massaged before they become normal again. I am inclined to think that such lecturers must be very few indeed, and ought rather to be classed with acrobats or gymnasts, than with professors of the essentially quiet and peaceful art of speaking in public. And yet I do not know. I have sometimes listened to public speakers whose efforts to make themselves heard and to vocalise their ideas involved them in a struggle that it was painful to witness, what it must have been for them to perform must be left to the imagination. The saddest thing about these contortions of mind and body is that the result of them is always in inverse proportion to the amount of muscular and mental effort expended upon them—indeed, I have several times been witness to a public speaker producing an entirely unintelligible roar, who in ordinary conversation was pleasant to listen to and quite easy to understand.

Unfortunately there are a large number of people who feel a fierce longing to teach their fellows vocally, who, although they have ideas in plenty, cannot realise at all that to make yourself heard intelligibly it is not merely useless, it is fatal to shout, that the only result of such folly is injury to the vocal organs, and that the complaint known as " clergyman's sore throat " is simply caused by not knowing how to use the voice. And here, although it is a digression (which I love) I will add that another very prevalent ailment known as " writer's cramp " or " pen paralysis " is caused not by the amount of writing done by the sufferer but through ignorance of the proper method of holding a pen while writing. Indeed, to see the way that most people hold a pen when writing is enough to induce wonder that their hands are not cramped without any writing but simply by holding the fingers in such an outrageous position.

I believe that voice production can be taught and that some people can learn it, but I know that some people whose vocation is public speaking are always painful to listen to and always give a sympathetic hearer the impression, true or false, that they are suffering very much also. With such people, if their matter is good, and it often is, this is a real affliction, and I condole with them very much, although I am grateful to say that I have never, since I began lecturing, had any difficulty in making myself heard distinctly, nor have I ever had a lesson in voice production. But I did have a long apprenticeship to open-air speaking and singing, some fifteen years altogether, and besides the inestimable practice thus gained, there was also the lesson, always to be learned from terrible examples, what to avoid.

Repeatedly secretaries and others have warned me that their hall was very bad for speaking in and on some occasions I have been told that no one had ever succeeded in making himself heard in a certain hall, but I can gratefully record the fact that I have never yet failed to make myself heard distinctly in every corner of the worst halls I have ever used for the purpose of lecturing. Yet some places, notably places of worship, are very trying to the voice, and after an hour and a half speaking in them there is a sense of weariness which is entirely absent after a similar effort in a good hall perhaps three times larger. This peculiarity of acoustics is, I believe, one of the chief trials of architects, and one that the greatest skill and care often fail to compete with successfully.

But I started this chapter with the idea of the exhaustion consequent upon a lecture. It varies, of course, according to the physical and mental fitness of the lecturer, but it is one of the most insidious forms of fatigue known. To the enthusiastic lecturer who rejoices in his task, and to whom it appears not only easy but natural and delightful, there is a strain upon the nerves that, unnoticed at the time, is severely felt afterwards. Just as some people feel a long train journey. " Surely," say the unthinking, " you cannot be tired after sitting for eight hours!" Can you not? I can answer for myself, who am a fairly good traveller, that it is almost as tiring as a day's manual labour, while many robust people it will make absolutely ill. And it is so with lecturing. In spite of the appearance of ease and the obvious delight of the lecturer in his work, it is using up his nerve force at a great rate, and he will do well to remember this afterwards, when those who have been listening to him often expect him to entertain them until midnight or after.

But there is another class of lecturer to whom every lecture is a tremendous ordeal. Gifted persons, with an ability to express themselves far above the average, the time that they are on their feet facing the audience may almost be described as a period of torture. What the interval of waiting for the time of the lecturer's beginning must mean to such unfortunate people I cannot tell, but I feel sure it must be agonising. I have heard one splendidly muscular friend of mine say that he would far rather do three days' heavy labour than give a couple of hours' reading from one of his books. And I have no choice but to believe him, the proof being that although the terms offered him were glittering enough he only endured for one season.

Unfortunately there are to be found folks who can neither make themselves heard nor say anything worth listening to if they could. I should think they have few nerves to speak of, or they could never survive one attempt to address an audience. Yet these are the very people who are the most anxious to be heard. In my open-air experience I suffered many things from them, because volunteers for that service are always eagerly welcomed, the rule being among most religious communities that if a man is fit for no other form of Christian service he will do to preach the Gospel in the open air. If any proof of this be needed it is only necessary to become an auditor at any open-air meeting for the propagation of the Gospel. The Salvation Army, which certainly does not follow the rule that anybody will do for the open air that is unfit for anything else, because all the members are called upon if willing, is no exception to the former rule. You will hear good speakers in the open-air meetings of the S.A., but—they are nearly always women. The men all seem to drop into a raucous, nauseous shout to which it is painful and entirely unprofitable to listen. The painful and pitiful thing is that people do listen, showing thereby that they have never heard any good speaking and so do not know how bad that is to which they are listening so intently.

I have taken the open-air preachers of the Gospel as my awful example, because of the splendid opportunities they daily and nightly waste through the ignorance of their leaders. If you want to hear good open-air speaking, listen to the Socialist orator, or the

Suffragette speaker. They have no use for the duffers, and so none are employed. I might go farther and say that they are in earnest—but I am afraid I shall be misunderstood. However, I cannot help it, I know it is as I say.

But the art of public speaking, simple as it may seem to be, is at a very low ebb. Go to any public function you like, nay, go to church, not chapel, and ask yourself what these people can be thinking of to stand up and try the nerves of their fellows with such mumblings and thought-mush. I know that there are some voices to which it is a sheer delight to listen, even if what they say is not worth hearing. At any rate, they do take the pains to make themselves audible, even if they cannot impart any useful information, and if it be in church it will hardly matter, because although all can hear, very few will heed, and unless the sermon is reported and gets into the press the preacher may say very nearly what he likes, and his congregation will not notice anything amiss.

Fortunately the " Platform," with a capital P, as lecturers love to designate their own special *métier*, is not at all likely to fail in making itself heard or understood. For in the first place, before a lecturer can hope to get anything like a decent fee or a sufficient number of engagements to-day he must have special qualifications, and especially he must speak so as to be heard and understood. Either he has made some subject peculiarly his own and is known as an authority upon that subject, or he is a traveller with special gifts of description and able to visualise the scenes he has witnessed for his audience, or he is a humorist, rarest and best gift of all. Were I offered my choice of a fairy's catalogue of offerings to men I would choose before all others the power of making men and women laugh—it takes but very little talent to make them weep—I had almost said that anyone can perform that sad feat. I look back upon the few occasions when in freakish mood I have got my audience laughing, and becoming imbued with their merry spirit have gone on in the same direction until we were all laughing together; I look back upon them, I say, as the golden hours of my life, hours that I rejoice to have lived and covet to live again, only that I know it to be impossible.

Let me recall one somewhat similar experience, but pray do not accuse me of irreverence in telling it since nothing can be farther from my thoughts. In the earlier days of my lecturing I often used to be engaged upon the understanding that I would preach in the local chapel or hall on the Sunday, the lecture being arranged for either Saturday or Monday night. On one such occasion I was booked to lecture in Scotland (never mind the town) on a certain Monday, on condition that I preached in the church the preceding morning and evening. From motives of economy, for it was in the early days, I travelled up by the night train, third class, and had the usual weary, cold, and sleepless experience consequent upon a winter night, spent in a corridor compartment with three others. I arrived at the church at about 9.30 and was shown by the caretaker into the vestry, where I had a wash and brush up and then laid down upon the sofa and went sound asleep.

Shortly after ten I was aroused by the pastor, and at first had some little difficulty in remembering where I was and what was expected of me. But the little rest had done wonders for me, and in a few minutes I felt quite ready for anything, my usual good spirits having fully returned. The pastor then timidly enquired what my subject would be for the morning's address, and I frankly replied that I did not know. My mind was a perfect blank as to topics, no new experience for me in such a position, since if I did prepare an address it was never of any use, never the one I delivered. He looked at me curiously when I told him this, thinking no doubt that I was treating my responsibilities with great levity, and then enquired if I had any wishes about the order of service. I told him that I wished he would do everything but the address.

At this he begged me most earnestly to let him off, telling me that he had been promising himself a rare treat and, well, he said many other things that I won't record for modesty's sake. These words had the effect of making me consent, and I selected the hymns, portions, etc., going into the pulpit a few minutes before the time in order to give the congregation what they always enjoy, a good look at the man who is going to address them, without their being able to reply, for half an hour or so. I sat in that elevated position looking straight down the church into the street, watching the people streaming in. And I got my subject—oh, yes, I got it splendidly. For the good folk approached the kirk door greeting one another with smiling faces, and pleasant words. In fact, all seemed as if the glorious morning had put them in the best of humours with all the world. And then they turned into the cool shade of the church door and a gloom fell upon their faces, I might reasonably say a blight, as if the news had just reached them of the loss of all they held dear. That sad frame persisted after they had taken their seats, in almost ludicrous contrast to the bright faces outside, still coming in and presently to assume the same lugubrious cast.

The voluntary ceased, the service commenced. I had chosen joyful hymns and psalms, but they were sung like dirges. At last I came to the sermon, and facing my audience squarely, without opening the Bible, said in a high, ecstatic voice,

"Oh, enter into His gates with thanksgiving,
And into His courts with praise."

Another pause, and then I went on to ask them in an easy, colloquial tone, smilingly, what was the matter with them. I spoke of the amazing contrast between their faces outside the building and within, and assumed that they had all been suddenly reminded of some poignant sorrow. And soon, with all the sarcasm I could muster, I lashed their assumed lugubriousness. They sat and stared as if uncertain whether they could possibly be hearing aright, and once a middle-aged man burst into an outrageous chuckle which very nearly infected the congregation. As I proceeded, the time flying all too rapidly, I had the satisfaction of seeing a natural expression beaming on all the faces, and when I concluded with the splendid words,

> "In His presence is fulness of joy!
> And at His right hand are pleasures for evermore,"

I could see that nothing but tradition, steel-hard tradition, prevented them from sending up a great shout of "Hallelujah."

Following me into the vestry, the pastor gripped me by both hands, saying:

"I would give a year of my life to be able to talk to my congregation like that. But, alas! it is impossible for many reasons. I shall never forget this morning though."

I laughed happily, for my present trouble was over, and replied:

"Nor I either. I've had a very enjoyable time. You see I'm a firm believer in the doctrine of "open thy mouth wide and I will fill it." I opened mine wide enough this morning, for surely there never was a poor wretch who had to speak to a waiting, critical assemblage emptier than I was. My head was like a bad nut, nothing in it but dust and shucks. And even now I don't know what I said, but your testimony and the look of the folks as they went out seem to tell me that it wasn't half bad, as the schoolboys say."

But somehow, owing, I suppose, to a certain freshness and unconventionality in treating the subject (I can safely say that now I shall never speak in public again), I was always a success as a preacher. Not, thank God, that I ever adopted the hat-on-back-of-the-head, cigar-in-mouth, hands-in-pocket style of preaching, so popular in the United States. Oh no, I had a far deeper idea of the sacredness of things than that. But there is a vast difference between solemnity and stupidity, and that is what many preachers do not seem to have found out yet.

The highest compliment upon my preaching that was ever paid me was at Dollar, a pleasant health resort near Edinburgh. I had been preaching in the Scotch Episcopal Church that morning, and I well remember energetically refusing to wear the black gown that the dear old minister fondly pressed upon me. As always, I did my best, but was not conscious of having excelled in any sense. On my way home to my host's house, however, in company with a very charming man, Mr. Robert Annan, I became aware of two small boys in Eton costume shyly waylaying me and endeavouring to catch my eye. I stopped, saying to Mr. Annan :

"I believe those boys want to speak to one of us."

He immediately turned to the boys, saying :

"Well, lads, what is it ? "

"Please, sir, we'd like to speak to Mr. Bullen."

"Certainly, my boys," I answered instantly, "go ahead."

"Are you going to preach again this evening, sir ? " said one of them, simply.

"I don't think so," I replied, "but suppose I was, what then ? "

"Well, sir," murmured the boy, looking down, "if you were, we wanted to come and hear you again."

Nothing that has ever been said to me or about me in connection with my oratorical efforts has ever given me such unmitigated delight as those few words, spoken, as I am convinced they must have been, with the most absolute sincerity. But it is quite unnecessary to enlarge upon them, their significance will be seen at once.

And now in order to close this chapter, already too long, let me say that there is a class of public speaker, fortunately very small, who neither in manner nor in matter is worth listening to, and yet these men will hold an otherwise intelligent audience, nay, will compel enthusiasm and subsequent adherence to the most fantastic or immoral of causes. I have in mind two such men, widely differing in personal character and aim but both indubitably possessed of this dangerous power, call it what one may. Some twelve years ago I stood in the Auditorium at Chicago and listened to John Alexander Dowie. I honestly declare that I never looked upon a less attractive man. In spite of his gorgeous robes (he was then posing as Elijah) all purple velvet and gold, his face and form were mean and contemptible, looking only fit for the taproom of a low public-house. And his address! It was beneath contempt. Poor shoddy, bad in delivery, sheer ungrammatical twaddle meaning nothing and leading nowhere. Yet his audience hung upon those banal words as if they had been the very oracles of God. In Heaven's name why?

The other man was Richard Seddon, Prime Minister of New Zealand. I attended a banquet given in his honour at the Australia Hotel, in Sydney, N.S.W., and sat among the élite of Southern journalism. Indeed, the company present was a thoroughly representative one, for the occasion was most important. I occupied the seat next but one to Mr. Seddon, and can honestly say that no guest there could be less biased than I was. I knew nothing of the man except common rumour, and that was entirely favourable. Yet before he spoke I was fascinated by the back of his head, which sloped forward from the neck without any "bulge" at all. In common parlance he had no back to his head. And I confess I felt doubtful. But when I heard him speak, and continue speaking for one hour and a quarter, I was aghast. I have heard a hundred times better matter from street-corner orators, in fact I have rarely listened to more turgid rubbish. The most astounding thing of all was that it literally hypnotised his audience. Had an archangel been addressing them they could not have shown wilder excitement, in fact whenever they got a chance they raved. And when the sorry performance was over I said to my friend next to me, the Editor of one of the great Sydney newspapers:

"In Heaven's name, what does all this mean? What is the matter with all these people?"

He had been just as bad as the rest, but he was now slightly ashamed of himself, I think, for he passed off my question diffidently and did not attempt to answer me. I could not call it turgid rhetoric, for it was not rhetoric, it was simply noisy rubbish, the few grains of sense that it contained being poured out within the first five minutes, and afterwards the whole perform-ance might well have been summed up in Shakespeare's immortal lines:

> "Like unto a tale told by an idiot, full of sound and fury,
> And signifying nothing."

CHAPTER XIX

ART OR APTITUDE

CHAPTER XIX

ART OR APTITUDE

AT the risk of being severely snubbed for my presumption I venture to add a few words for the benefit of that numerous class of persons who feel an intense desire to address their fellows, but either do not possess the confidence or ability to do so. But I do realise the great difficulty of advising such people, because I am fully persuaded that there are many of them that will never be able to address an audience with any satisfaction to themselves or benefit to their hearers. And there are others who will never have any difficulty beyond the commencement. Nature has fitted them for public speakers, and the only thing necessary to their complete equipment is that they shall be thoroughly acquainted with their subject.

Now I am well aware that elocution and voice production are taught both by book and voice, but I do not know anything of the results. It has never been my lot knowingly to listen to a public speaker who has studied elocution as an art, but I may have done so unknowingly. I have, however, listened to men with a high reputation as public speakers, and have wondered mightily how anybody, not compelled thereto by any cause, could endure them for five minutes. And I have listened with sheer delight to others whom I have known to be men and women who had never even given a thought to training their voice or their gestures, but who were filled with intense love and knowledge of their subject, who apparently had only to open their mouths and let the stream of eloquence flow.

Of course; and therein lies, I fully believe, the prime principle and art of public speaking. At the same time I do fully recognise that there is a third great class between the two I have mentioned who without a little training or a little encouragement will never deliver the message they undoubtedly possess. Shyness, indolence, want of confidence in themselves: these are all heavy handicaps against a budding public speaker, and it is for such as these that I would speak now.

In the first place, I would say get rid of self-consciousness. Do not dare to allow yourself to think of your personal appearance. If you haven't done your best for that in the solitude of your dressing-room before your mirror you are hopeless, but if you have, and then continue to wonder how you are appearing to the audience, you are equally hopeless. Forget your appearance and believe what is undoubtedly true, that if your message is worth listening to, all the better part of the audience are attending to it and are not caring a bit what you look like. At one of the most successful meetings I have ever had, one side of my dress-shirt front had a big patch of oil on it, which compared most strangely with the immaculate whiteness of the other half. My chest was very queer, and I wore a chest-protector which I had too liberally sprinkled with camphorated oil. This had come through my vest and spoiled my shirt-front. But I didn't know anything about it until the affair was over, and then I realised that my audience didn't know either, or if they did, it hadn't affected their enthusiasm.

Of course, I do not in the least mean to suggest or imply that a speaker should be careless of or neglect his or her personal appearance ; on the contrary, I regard it as a duty to the audience you have the honour to address that you should appear as neat and trim as possible without showing yourself eccentric or bizarre. Any fool can do that, and I may add with conviction that only fools will try by means of long hair and quaint clothing to attract the attention they could not gain otherwise. Of course, there are exceptions even to this rule. But what I do mean is that no public speaker, having dressed decently and reasonably, should thenceforth think about his appearance but should devote the entire powers of his mind to the service of his audience.

In the second place I would advise all young speakers to cultivate unconsciousness of their audience as individuals. Rather look upon and think of them as one individual with whom you are going to have an earnest confidential chat. While always cultivating that cosy air of confidence and conversational manner, beware of becoming slipshod, slangy or allusive. I know that this sounds like a counsel of perfection, but I know too how greatly it is needed. For although I hate the ultra-pessimistic assumed by so many middle-aged men with regard to manners and customs in general, it is impossible to avoid the conclusion that among reasonably intelligent men of the " hupper suckles " present-day conversation is largely made up of " I meantersay, dontcherknow " and " what ! " (explosive). And, alas ! the upper middle-class do ape this detestable habit. I have heard men, occupying responsible positions, whose conversation was quite unintelligible from this cause, and I could only think that they used the idiotic convention because they did not want to talk—I knew that they were highly intelligent.

A great friend of mine, who was at the time managing director of a great Australasian newspaper, visited me some years ago and his comments upon this habit among our otherwise intelligent classes were continual and lurid.

" It seems to me," he would say, " that the men I meet in England to-day have never learned how to talk, or else they have nothing to say. Their whole conversation seems to be made up of a few misapplied adverbs such as ' frightfully, beastly, awfully ' and

'well, I meantersay, doncherknow' and 'hwhatt!'
They drive me nearly crazy, and only that I do occasionally find a man who talks rationally I would not
stop in the country another day."

I told him what I gratefully acknowledged to be the
fact, that the people of whom he complained, though
a far too numerous class, are but the fringe of the
intelligence of the nation. Still it may not be denied
that in spite of reason and nature, both men and
women of education and high position do cultivate
this maddening convention. I certainly would not
have dealt with it at the length I have were it not that
I have advised a conversational manner with an
audience, and I must make it clear that I mean conversation and not the silly ejaculations I have noted
above.

And notwithstanding this real drawback I maintain
that where a speaker can get upon those confidential
conversational terms with his hearers he is absolutely
sure of their attention, sure too of conveying his meaning to their minds. His speech will not be oratory.
That may at once be admitted. Oratory has its
distinct uses, its well-defined place, but it is not for
teaching or amusement. It belongs to great occasions
and to great orators. To the ordinary successful
speaker or preacher it is like the panoply of Saul
upon the immature shoulders of David. There may
come occasions when the successful speaker will rise
to the sublime heights of oratory and carry his audience

with him in a torrent of enthusiasm, but with those peaks we have not to deal, we are discussing the high road.

Next I would say, avoid all mannerisms of speech or gesture as you would suggestions of the evil one. I once was told by a gentleman who had heard me lecturing that I used rather too frequently the phrase " as a matter of fact." I am afraid I was not at all grateful, I know that I flushed hotly, but I have since often recalled that quiet remark as one of the most valuable hints I ever received. For thenceforth I was on my guard, and if I found myself (as I often did) rolling a certain expression caressingly under my tongue I immediately set a watch for it and ruthlessly cut it out. Gesture is another pitfall for some people. It cannot be taught satisfactorily, although rules for its use are in all the books. I believe that the only effective gesture is the natural one—any gesture that you have to learn and practise up is unnatural, stilted, and stagey. That last word may be misunderstood ; let me explain what I mean. All great actors are nearly natural in their gestures, those who miss greatness, those whom it is right to call theatrical are not. The late Rev. Joseph Parker was an actor and a very poor one ; to my mind some of his theatricalities on the City Temple platform would have got him hissed off the stage. I have known him drop his voice until he was entirely inaudible, at the same time solemnly wagging his great head from side to side, then suddenly bounding forward with impassioned gesture he would roar like a lion. It was all stagey and transpontine, but the magnetism of the man carried it off triumphantly and the people to whom he preached felt that he was the first of preachers and the rest nowhere.

In all of the foregoing I have assumed that you whom I am advising have a good voice and have had some practice in using it. There may be, yes, I remember that there are, some people who will try to speak from a public platform without possessing that first requisite, a voice. But I am not talking to idiots, but ordinarily sensible men and women who are able to make themselves heard at a considerable distance without shouting. If they have not had the opportunity as I had for fifteen years of practising the art, I suppose I may call it, of voice production in the open air, let them go to a professor of elocution, who will teach them so to use their voices that they will not have clergyman's sore throat at the end of a short address, and feel as if they can never speak again.

When I tell you that I bear the burden of chronic laryngitis, and have done for a quarter of a century, yet never have known a " tired " throat or a clergyman's sore throat, I am sure that if you believe me you will admit that practice has done great things for me. I have lectured with an ulcerated throat, with a severe cold, with influenza ; lectured when the pain of inflammation in my throat was almost maddening; but never once can I honestly say that speaking had anything to do with my sufferings. Indeed, I have usually gone on addressing audiences each night until quite well, although told at the beginning by medical men that to address an audience in my then condition amounted to suicide.

Now this must be owing to my practical knowledge of voice production. I cannot teach it, I wish I could, because it would help my meagre finances very much just now, but I know it, and if it were necessary I could produce a great cloud of witnesses to the fact. People who have seen me crawling gaspingly up the steps of a lecture hall apparently unable to speak. One of the commonest remarks I remember during the last three or four years of my lecturing was :

" Why, Mr. Bullen, you'll never be able to lecture to-night ! " But I always was, and I am grateful to recall that I never broke an engagement for that cause, although I know that at the last I ran it very fine indeed, because I could hardly speak for coughing. But the ordinary individual with a good voice must be taught in some way how to produce it, or he will never make an efficient speaker, never be able to hit the happy mean between shouting and whispering, the audible mean between two forms of unintelligibility.

Throughout it will be noticed that I have assumed a complete knowledge of the subject in hand on the part of the would-be lecturer. That would seem to go without saying, yet strangely enough it does not. It is passing strange that any man should dream of addressing an audience upon a topic about which it is dollars to doughnuts that they know as much or more than he does, yet there are such people. Of course, they do not go very far, still they exist. One such asked me if I would kindly lend him my notes (I never had any, by the way) of the whaling lecture, and the negatives of my slides, as he felt sure he could work up quite a nice little connection for himself in South Wales. It was a subject he said that had always interested him very much. I know this hardly sounds true, but it is actually so in every detail.

Assuming then as I do that the would-be lecturer knows his subject thoroughly, in what style should he deliver an address thereupon? This is a matter upon which I hold very strong views. To copy anyone else's style is fatal, to strain after effect equally so, and I am firmly of opinion that the only sensible plan is to tell your story naturally as if you were just yarning to a chum. In doing so, however, one must bear in mind all that I have said before, or else the talk will be a jumble. It is little short of delightful to sit and listen to a speaker who is telling you strange facts in an easy, confidential, colloquial manner, compelling you to strain neither your hearing nor intellect, but interesting you in spite of yourself; interesting you you so much that when the end is suddenly reached you start with amazement, hardly able to believe that you have been listening for an hour and thirty or forty minutes, so rapidly and easily has the time flown.

Here I feel moved to interpolate a remark which does not really apply to the learner or beginner, but to men who are very fluent and enthusiastic. Gentlemen, forgive me for saying so, but the human brain is like a sponge, it will only hold so much at a time; afterwards you can pour as much liquid as you like on it, it will not absorb another drop. Also the average listener's attention with the best of intentions will flag after ninety minutes at the outside, much quicker than that if he or she has a train to catch. I have often heard it said:

" Oh, yes, I like Mr. So-and-so very much for the first hour and a half, after that I feel that I want to kill him. I'll never go to hear him again."

For your own sakes, gentlemen, do not allow that to be said of you. Do not let the curse of not knowing how to leave off descend upon you and mar fatally what is otherwise your very delightful performance. You may possibly think me unfit to advise you upon this or any other subject, you may indignantly deny that you ever were or could be guilty of overstaying your welcome, but you cannot imagine that in being thus emphatic I have any other object in view than your good. And this is especially the case as regards the beginner. When a man is always well received, finds his audiences enthusiastic and listens to incessant eulogies upon himself and his messages, then he needs especially to keep his eye upon his watch. Never tire your auditors is an excellent rule, and I am perfectly certain that more harm has been done to themselves by individual lecturers in this way than in any other that can be mentioned.

I must end this chapter as I began it by humbly disclaiming any idea of presumption. I do not arrogate to myself any title to instruct except that conferred by experience and success. But I will add that I do not think that any man, however great his other qualifications as a public speaker may be, can possibly succeed as a lecturer unless he enjoys his work, unless he is able to feel that glorious thrill of sympathy emanating from his audience lifting him on to a far higher plane than he could ever reach otherwise. When he sees all those rows of faces with their hundreds of eyes uplifted to him and realises that he for the moment at any rate is the centre of attraction—well, I repeat, if this does not inspire him and lift him out of himself I would give very little for his elocution or knowledge or steadiness of nerve.

Of course, the highest form of all, when the message must be delivered at whatever personal cost, is only possible to a few of us, and is moreover not at all necessary for the equipment of a professional lecturer. Amazing though it may seem, we do, in spite of so many repetitions, maintain a great enthusiasm for our various messages, nor can anyone say truthfully that such enthusiasm is manufactured or, in vulgar parlance, pumped up. But even that is seen at its best where aptitude has been assisted by art to present the message in the most acceptable form to an eager audience.

CHAPTER XX

SUMMING UP

CHAPTER XX

SUMMING UP

AS I draw near to the close of this book I feel profoundly sad. There comes over me a feeling like that of the invalid who takes to his bed knowing that he will leave his room no more until he is carried out. For I feel that I am now closing the door behind me upon a profession which with all its manifold delights I did not enter upon until middle age, and did not lay down until physical disability rendered it impossible to carry it on any longer. I have never enjoyed anything more than lecturing, except in America, where I felt that the people might as well sit and chew gum anywhere else as sit there stolidly before me and do so. For although in Great Britain and Australasia I was always able to get on good terms with my audiences immediately I never did succeed in doing so in America, and so that was the only lecture season of which I grew thoroughly tired. Yet my experience may be strictly personal; I have reason to believe that other men have fared far differently—some, indeed, find it impossible to fill all the lecture engagements they receive there and make very large sums of money. I would rather then say that the fault is with me—some subtle want of sympathy with the American character which reflects upon myself in coldness and inattention.

Another matter upon which I must make a few remarks to avoid misunderstanding is the avoidance in these pages of names, except in a very few instances. I have purposely omitted names of fellow-lecturers because I could not speak of them all from personal knowledge, and I would not for the world cause any heart-burnings. It would be a pity, for I firmly believe that lecturers as a class are the best of good fellows, and never speak of each other but in the highest terms of eulogy. They are naturally of many different talents, each a specialist in his way, not all equally excellent or equally successful, that need hardly be said, but all animated not only by a desire to please their public, but to help one another. All of us have felt sincere difficulty when asked by those who have the direction of societies and selection of lectures which of our colleagues we would recommend for a succeeding season. It is a tactless question, of course, but that does not make the answer easier, and we are often driven to some quaint subterfuges in reply. But when the secretary says, " We have got Mr. or Professor or Miss —— coming for the next lecture," we get our opportunity, and I know from much pleasant experience how eagerly those occasions are seized and made full use of by all of us. And it is very pleasant too—brings out the best that is in us.

Sitting here beyond these voices I rejoice to have none but pleasant recollections of those who were on the " platform " at the same time as I was, of their helpfulness and good-fellowship. Of course, we have all felt considerable annoyance at the intrusion into the lecture sphere of the big fellows to whom money was no object—they had already more than enough of that—who could not want occupation, for Heaven knows they were busy enough, and we could not help feeling that to those of us whose lecturing was our business, our main support, they were not playing the game. In fact, they were what the Trade Unionist would call blacklegs, and with far greater reason than he ever uses the term.

And there were, nay there are others, not those who give up their hard-won evenings to lecture to needy little societies, content if they may only do some good and never asking for any recognition either in money or praise, oh no, but those in high places whose names will command an audience and who take money they do not need from those who do. But except among ourselves we do not growl about these things. I should not, were I still on the job ; it's only because I am now on the further shore that I venture to say what has long been in my mind. It has always seemed to me the sheerest injustice that any man who is already earning a good income at a profession should butt into another profession on the strength of his name and take from its genuine professors so much of their hard earnings. But I suppose there will always be a diversity of view upon this point, so I merely give mine for what it may be worth ; I ask no one to accept it.

But of those who belong to the inner circle whose names as I write rise before me like welcome ghosts, how gladly would I, if it were permissible, tell of your kindness to me on many occasions. That is out of the question, however, because I do not know you all equally well, and therefore I should be driven to make an unconscious selection which would never do. I therefore speak in general terms, but only from necessity of avoiding all appearance of discrimination, not because I have any favourites.

As I sit here and muse of the few and stormy years of my past life I remember with something approaching mild surprise how very easily I have taken the many great changes that have overtaken me. Only the first, when I was suddenly flung into a harsh and cruel world from the sheltered haven of my aunt's quiet home at the age of eight and a half, was received by me with a storm of bitter grief. I remember how fiercely I wept as I have never done before or since, and I now know that could I but have foreseen what the next few years held in store for me I should probably not have survived that sad night.

Then came at eleven and a half the sudden change from Street Arab to Sea Waif, accepted with a philosophical calm that might have been expected, I admit.

Fifteen years later in my young manhood came the great change from being first mate of a ship to holding a junior clerkship ashore. Now that change by all the rules should have been the hardest of all to bear calmly, but I protest that it came to me as one of the most natural of transitions, and I never felt the slightest desire to go to sea again. Only sometimes on a Saturday night, when my means were all too small to furnish the Londoner's sacrament, a nice Sunday dinner for the family, I sighed for the irresponsible days at sea where Saturday night was no different from any other night in the week, for our bread was given us and our water was sure, even if both were poor in quality and scanty in quantity.

Then came the great and momentous change at forty-two of resigning my two-pound-a-week clerkship and embarking upon the stormy sea of journalism and authorship. Late, very late in life, and indeed too late to give me much joy, for the iron of poverty and struggle, of scorn and failure had entered into my very soul. And to crown all, my youngest son, my Benjamin, had died on the very day that my first book was accepted. But such joy as I could feel I did. All my new acquaintances and friends bade me welcome, helped me, said nice things about me, and I earned a good deal of money. I paid all my debts and enjoyed to the full what I had long sighed for, the power to pay cash for everything as I received it, and the full determination that if possible to do so should always be my rule while I lived. Most gratefully do I declare that so far that rule has been realised.

But the change was easy, I felt no strangeness about it any more than I had ever done since the first. And yet it was as great a change as a man could well experience and live. Now, however, I have come to another change which I feel is the final one, except, of course, the closing of the book to which all of us must come. And as through this month of November I sit by my fireside I do feel as I have never done before, a sense of loss, of having looked my last upon the multitude of friends I made while lecturing. I find myself recalling the upturned faces in their serried rows, the bursts of applause, the involuntary remarks made by some enthusiastic listener, the sense of power for good in that I was interesting and amusing many of my fellow-creatures by whom I should be remembered for many and many a day. Yes, even to their lives' end, for although thirty years have passed since I heard J. Jackson Wray lecture, his image, his voice, his words are all as vivid to me now as they were on that night in Sutherland Gardens Chapel when I sat entranced to hear him.

And in like manner my heart has been rejoiced to be greeted in Australia, in South America, in India, in Canada, by some friendly voice telling me of keen recollections of my lecture at some place or another long before. Now I often sit and think with mellow happiness that scattered all over the world there are people who are thinking kindly of me to-night as of one who spoke words to them pleasant to recall, and the thought does in some measure compensate me for my very great loss.

Yes, this is the greatest change of all, and the hardest to bear, and that is principally why I have again taken up my now seldom used pen, to recall and set down many of the well-remembered incidents of my life and to bid all who loved me and knew me as a lecturer a quiet but tender

FAREWELL

VOL. II.

Human Anatomy for Art Students

BY

SIR ALFRED D. FRIPP, K.C.V.O., C.B., M.B., M.S. (Lond.), F.R.C.S.

Surgeon-in-Ordinary to H.M. the King; Lecturer upon Anatomy at Guy's Hospital, London

AND

RALPH THOMPSON, M.B., Ch.M., F.R.C.S. (Eng.)

Senior Demonstrator of Anatomy, Guy's Hospital

And an Appendix on Comparative Anatomy, and Illustrations, by
HARRY DIXON, M.S.B.S.

Profusely Illustrated with Photographs, and by Drawings by
INNES FRIPP, A.R.C.A.

Master of Life Class, City Guilds Art School

With 151 Illustrations. Square extra crown 8vo. 7s. 6d. net

"An ideal manual for the student of the most difficult and most essential branch of art study."
Liverpool Daily Post.

"This book, with its abundant and excellent illustrations, will be a real help to knowledge."
Pall Mall Gazette.

"Excellently illustrated from the first page to the last by original drawings and photographs most carefully taken."—*Westminster Gazette.*

"Combines the best scientific and artistic information."—*Connoisseur.*

"A book which we can unhesitatingly recommend to the art student, because it is written by men who are thoroughly at home in the subject treated of, and who, moreover, have been mindful not to encumber their exposition with unnecessary minutiæ."—*Studio.*

VOL. III.

Modelling and Sculpture

BY

ALBERT TOFT, A.R.C.A., M.S.B.S.

Profusely Illustrated with Photographs and Drawings

Square extra crown 8vo., 6s. net. With 119 Illustrations

"The details are very clearly set out, and the instruction throughout is of a thoroughly practical kind."—*Nottingham Guardian.*

"A model of clearness. A book that should be found most attractive to all art lovers, as well as invaluable to students of the processes described therein."—*School Guardian.*

"Will be exceedingly useful and even indispensable to all who wish to learn the art of sculpture in its many branches. The book will also appeal to those who have no intention of learning the art, but wish to know something about it. Mr. Toft writes very clearly."—*Field.*

"Written in a most interesting manner, beautifully printed on excellent paper, and illustrated as Messrs. Seeley know how to illustrate."—*Glasgow Citizen.*

"Will be found an invaluable aid to the student. . . . Takes the student step by step through the various technical processes, the text being supplemented by over a hundred excellent illustrations."—*Studio.*

SEELEY, SERVICE & CO. LIMITED

A Catalogue of Books on Art, History, and General Literature Published by Seeley, Service & Co Ltd. 38 Great Russell St. London

Some of the Contents

Crown Library, The 4
Elzevir Library, The 5
Events of Our Own Times Series . . 6
Illuminated Series, The 8
Miniature Library of Devotion, The . . 9
Miniature Portfolio Monographs, The . 9
Missions, The Library of 10
New Art Library, The 11
Portfolio Monographs 11
Science of To-Day Series, The . . . 14
Seeley's Illustrated Pocket Library . . 14
Seeley's Standard Library 15
Story Series, The 15
"Things Seen" Series, The . . . 16

The Publishers will be pleased to post their complete Catalogue or their Illustrated Miniature Catalogue on receipt of a post-card

CATALOGUE OF BOOKS

*Arranged alphabetically under the names of
Authors and Series*

ABBOTT, Rev. E. A., D.D.
How to Parse. An English Grammar. Fcap. 8vo, 3s. 6d.
How to Tell the Parts of Speech. An Introduction to English
Grammar. Fcap. 8vo, 2s.
How to Write Clearly. Rules and Exercises on English Composition. 1s. 6d.
Latin Gate, The. A First Latin Translation Book. Crown 8vo, 3s. 6d.
Via Latina. A First Latin Grammar. Crown 8vo, 3s. 6d.

ABBOTT, Rev. E. A., and Sir J. R. SEELEY.
English Lessons for English People. Crown 8vo, 4s. 6d.

ADY, Mrs. *See* CARTWRIGHT, JULIA.

À KEMPIS, THOMAS.
Of the Imitation of Christ. With Illuminated Frontispiece and Title
Page, and Illuminated Sub-Titles to each book. In white or blue cloth, with inset minia-
tures. Gilt top; crown 8vo, 6s. nett; also bound in same manner in real classic vellum.
Each copy in a box, 10s. 6d. nett; Antique leather with clasps, 10s. 6d. nett.
"It may well be questioned whether the great work of Thomas à Kempis has
ever been presented to better advantage."—*The Guardian.*

ANDERSON, Prof. W.
Japanese Wood Engravings. Coloured Illustrations. Super-royal 8vo,
sewed, 2s. 6d. nett; half-linen, 3s. 6d. nett; also small 4to, cloth, 2s. nett; lambskin, 3s. nett.

ARMSTRONG, Sir WALTER.
The Art of Velazquez. Illustrated. Super-royal 8vo, 3s. 6d. nett.
The Life of Velazquez. Illustrated. Super-royal 8vo, 3s. 6d. nett.
Velazquez. A Study of his Life and Art. With Eight Copper Plates and
many minor Illustrations. Super-royal 8vo, cloth, 9s. nett.
Thomas Gainsborough. Illustrated. Super-royal 8vo, half-linen, 3s. 6d.
nett. Also new edition small 4to, cloth, 2s. nett; leather, 3s. nett and 5s. nett.
The Peel Collection and the Dutch School of Painting. With Illustra-
tions in Photogravure and Half-tone. Super-royal 8vo, sewed, 5s. nett; cloth, 7s. nett.
W. Q. Orchardson. Super-royal 8vo, sewed, 2s. 6d.; half-linen, 3s. 6d. nett.

AUGUSTINE, S.
Confessions of S. Augustine. With Illuminated pages. In white or
blue cloth, gilt top, crown 8vo, 6s. nett; also in vellum, 10s. 6d. nett.

BAKER, Captain B. GRANVILLE
The Passing of the Turkish Empire in Europe. With Thirty-two
Illustrations. Demy 8vo, 16s. nett.

BARING-GOULD, Rev. S.
Family Names and their Story. Demy 8vo, 7s. 6d. nett. 5s. nett.

BEDFORD, Rev. W. K. R.
Malta and the Knights Hospitallers. Super-royal 8vo, sewed, 2s. 6d.
nett; half-linen, 3s. 6d. nett.

BENHAM, Rev. Canon D. D., F.S.A.
The Tower of London. With Four Plates in Colours and many other
Illustrations. Super-royal 8vo, sewed, 5s. nett; cloth, 7s. nett.
Mediæval London. With a Frontispiece in Photogravure, Four Plates
in Colour, and many other Illustrations. Super-royal 8vo, sewed, 5s. nett; cloth, gilt
top, 7s. nett. Also extra crown 8vo, 3s. 6d. nett.
Old St. Paul's Cathedral. With a Frontispiece in Photogravure, Four
Plates printed in Colour, and many other Illustrations. Super-royal 8vo, sewed, 5s. nett,
or cloth, gilt top, 7s. nett.

BENNETT, EDWARD.
The Post Office and its Story. An interesting account of the activities
of a great Government department. With Twenty-five Illustrations. Ex. crn. 8vo, 5s. nett.

BICKERSTETH, Rev. E.
Family Prayers for Six Weeks. Crown 8vo, 3s. 6d.
A Companion to the Holy Communion. 32mo, cloth, 1s.

Seeley, Service & Co Limited

BINYON, LAURENCE.

Dutch Etchers of the Seventeenth Century. Illustrated. Super-royal 8vo, sewed, 2s. 6d. ; half-linen, 3s. 6d. nett.

John Crome and John Sell Cotman. Illustrated. Super-royal 8vo, sewed, 3s. 6d. nett.

BIRCH, G. H.

London on Thames in Bygone Days. With Four Plates printed in Colour and many other Illustrations. Super-royal 8vo, sewed, 5s. nett ; cloth, 7s. nett.

BRIDGES, Rev. C.

An Exposition of Psalm CXIX. Crown 8vo, 5s.

BUTCHER, E. L.

Things Seen in Egypt. With Fifty Illustrations. Small 4to, cloth, 2s. nett ; lambskin, 3s. nett ; velvet leather, in box, 5s. nett.

CACHEMAILLE, Rev. E. P., M.A.

XXVI Present-Day Papers on Prophecy. An explanation of the visions of Daniel and of the Revelation, on the continuous historic system. With Maps and Diagrams. 700 pp. 6s. nett.

CARTWRIGHT, JULIA.

Jules Bastien-Lepage. Super-royal 8vo, sewed, 2s. 6d. ; cloth, 3s. 6d. nett.

Sacharissa. Some Account of Dorothy Sidney, Countess of Sunderland, her Family and Friends. With Five Portraits. Demy 8vo, 7s. 6d.

Raphael in Rome. Illustrated. Super-royal 8vo, sewed, 2s. 6d. ; half-linen, 3s. 6d. nett ; also in small 4to, cloth, 2s. nett ; leather, 3s. nett and 5s. nett.

The Early Work of Raphael. Illustrated. Super-royal 8vo, sewed 2s. 6d. ; half-linen, 3s. 6d. Also new edition, revised, in small 4to, in cloth, 2s. nett ; leather, 3s. nett.

Raphael : A Study of his Life and Work. With Eight Copper Plates and many other Illustrations. Super-royal 8vo, 7s. 6d. nett.

CESARESCO, The Countess MARTINENGO

The Liberation of Italy. With Portraits on Copper. Crown 8vo, 5s.

CHATTERTON, E. KEBLE.

Fore and Aft. The Story of the Fore and Aft Rig from the Earliest Times to the Present Day. Sq. ex. royal 8vo. With 150 Illustrations and Coloured Frontispiece by C. DIXON, R.I. 16s. nett.

Through Holland in the "Vivette." The Cruise of a 4-Tonner from the Solent to the Zuyder Zee, through the Dutch Waterways. With Sixty Illustrations and Charts, 6s. nett.

CHITTY, J. R.

Things Seen in China. With Fifty Illustrations. Cloth, 2s. nett ; leather, 3s. nett ; velvet leather in a box, 5s. nett.

CHORAL SERVICE-BOOK FOR PARISH CHURCHES, THE.

Compiled and Edited by J. W. ELLIOTT, Organist and Choirmaster of St. Mark's, Hamilton Terrace, London. With some Practical Counsels taken by permission from "Notes on the Church Service," by Bishop WALSHAM HOW.

A. Royal 8vo, sewed, 1s. ; cloth, 1s. 6d.
B. 16mo, sewed, 6d. ; cloth, 8d.

The following portions may be had separately :—

The Ferial and Festal Responses and the Litany. Arranged by J. W. ELLIOTT. Sewed, 4d.

The Communion Service, Kyrie, Credo, Sanctus, and Gloria in Excelsis. Set to Music by Dr. J. NAYLOR, Organist of York Minster. Sewed, 4d.

Seeley, Service & Co Limited

CHURCH, Sir ARTHUR H., F.R.S.
Josiah Wedgwood, Master Potter. With many Illustrations. Super-royal 8vo, sewed, 5s. nett; cloth, 7s. nett; also small 4to, cloth, 2s. nett; leather, 3s. and 5s. nett.
The Chemistry of Paints and Painting. Third Edition. Crown 8vo, 6s.

CHURCH, Rev. A. J.
Nicias, and the Sicilian Expedition. Crown 8vo, 1s. 6d.
For other books by Professor CHURCH see Complete Catalogue.

CLARK, J. W., M.A.
Cambridge. With a coloured Frontispiece and many other Illustrations by A. BRUNET-DEBAINES and H. TOUSSAINT, &c. Extra crown 8vo, 6s.; also crown 8vo, cloth, 2s. nett; leather, 3s.; special leather, in box, 5s. nett.

CODY, Rev. H. A.
An Apostle of the North. The Biography of the late Bishop BOMPAS, First Bishop of Athabasca, and with an Introduction by the ARCHBISHOP of RUPERTS-LAND. With 42 Illustrations. Demy 8vo, 7s. 6d. nett. 5s. nett.

CORBIN, T. W.
Engineering of To-day. With Seventy-three Illustrations and Diagrams. Extra crown 8vo, 5s. nett.
Mechanical Inventions of To-Day. Ex. crown 8vo; with Ninety-four Illustrations, 5s. nett.

CORNISH, C. J.
Animals of To-day: Their Life and Conversation. With Illustrations from Photographs by C. REID of Wishaw. Crown 8vo, 6s.
The Isle of Wight. Illustrated. Super-royal 8vo, sewed, 2s. 6d. nett; half-linen, 3s. 6d. nett; also a new edition, small 4to, cloth, 2s. nett; leather, 3s. nett and 5s. nett.
Life at the Zoo. Notes and Traditions of the Regent's Park Gardens. Illustrated from Photographs by GAMBIER BOLTON. Fifth Edition. Crown 8vo, 6s.
The Naturalist on the Thames. Many Illustrations. Demy 8vo, 7s. 6d.
The New Forest. Super-royal 8vo, sewed, 2s. 6d. nett; half-linen, 3s. 6d. nett; also new edition, small 4to, cloth, 2s.; leather, 3s. nett; and special velvet leather, each copy in a box, 5s.
The New Forest and the Isle of Wight. With Eight Plates and many other Illustrations. Super-royal 8vo, 7s. 6d. nett.
Nights with an Old Gunner, and other Studies of Wild Life. With Sixteen Illustrations by LANCELOT SPEED, CHARLES WHYMPER, and from Photographs. Crown 8vo, 6s.

THE CROWN LIBRARY

A series of notable copyright books issued in uniform binding.
Extra crown 8vo. With many illustrations, 5s. nett.

RECENTLY ISSUED.

SWANN, A. J.
Fighting the Slave Hunters in Central Africa. A Record of Twenty-six Years of Travel and Adventure round the Great Lakes, and of the overthrow of Tip-pu-Tib, Rumaliza, and other great Slave Traders. With 45 Illustrations and a Map, 5s. nett.

GRUBB, W. BARBROOKE.
An Unknown People in an Unknown Land. An Account of the Life and Customs of the Lengua Indians of the Paraguayan Chaco, with Adventures and Experiences met with during Twenty Years' Pioneering and Exploration amongst them. With Twenty-four Illustrations and a Map. Extra crown 8vo, 5s. nett.

FRASER, Sir A. H. L., K.C.S.I., M.A., LL.D., Litt.D., ex-Lieutenant-Governor of Bengal.
Among Indian Rajahs and Ryots. A Civil Servants' Recollections and Impressions of Thirty-seven Years of Work and Sport in the Central Provinces and Bengal. Third Edition, 5s. nett.

Seeley, Service & Co Limited

CODY, Rev. H. A.

    An Apostle of the North. The Story of Bishop Bompas's Life amongst the Red Indians & Eskimo. Third Edition, 5s. nett.

PENNELL, T. L., M.D., B.Sc.

    Among the Wild Tribes of the Afghan Frontier. A Record of Sixteen Years' close intercourse with the natives of Afghanistan and the North-West Frontier Introduction by EARL ROBERTS. Extra crown 8vo. Twenty-six Illustrations and Map Fifth Edition, 5s. net.

CUST, LIONEL.

    The Engravings of Albert Dürer. Illustrated. Super-royal 8vo, half-linen, 3s. 6d. nett.

    Paintings and Drawings of Albert Dürer. Illustrated. Super-royal 8vo, sewed, 3s. 6d. nett.

    Albrecht Dürer. A Study of his Life and Work. With Eight Copper Plates and many other Illustrations. Super-royal 8vo, 7s. 6d.

DAVENPORT, CYRIL.

    Cameos. With examples in Colour and many other Illustrations. Super-royal 8vo, sewed, 5s. nett; cloth, 7s. nett.

    Royal English Bookbindings. With Coloured Plates and many other Illustrations. Super-royal 8vo, sewed, 3s. 6d.; cloth, 4s. 6d.

DAVIES, RANDALL, F.S.A.

    English Society of the Eighteenth Century in Contemporary Art. With Four Coloured and many other Illustrations. Super royal 8vo, sewed, 5s. nett; cloth, 7s. nett.

DAWSON, Rev. E. C.

    The Life of Bishop Hannington. Crown 8vo, paper boards, 2s. 6d.; or with Map and Illustrations, cloth, 3s. 6d.

DESTRÉE, O. G.

    The Renaissance of Sculpture in Belgium. Illustrated. Super-royal 8vo, sewed, 2s. 6d. nett; half-linen, 3s. 6d. nett.

DOLMAGE, CECIL G., M.A., D.C.L., LL.D., F.R.A.S.

    Astronomy of To-Day. A popular account in non-technical language. With Forty-six Illustrations and Diagrams. Extra crown 8vo, 5s. nett.

DOMVILLE-FIFE, CHARLES W.

    Submarine Engineering of To-Day. Extra crown 8vo, 5s. nett.

DRACOPOLI, I. N., F.R.G.S.

    Through Jubaland to the Lorian Swamp. Forty-four Illustrations and Two Maps, 16s. nett.

ELZEVIR LIBRARY, THE.

    Selections from the choicest English Writers. Exquisitely Illustrated, with Frontispiece and Title-page in Colours by H. M. BROCK, and many other Illustrations. Half bound in cloth, coloured top, 1s. nett; full leather, 1s. 6d. nett; velvet leather, gilt edges, in a box, 2s. 6d. nett.

Volume I. Fancy & Humour of Lamb.	Volume VI. Vignettes of London Life from Dickens.
„ II. Wit & Imagination of Disraeli.	
„ III. Vignettes from Oliver Goldsmith.	„ VII. XVIIIth Century Vignettes from Thackeray.
„ IV. Wit & Sagacity of Dr. Johnson.	„ VIII. Vignettes of Country Life from Dickens.
„ V. Insight & Imagination of John Ruskin.	„ IX. Wisdom & Humour of Carlyle.

    "Decidedly natty and original in get-up."—*The Saturday Review.*

EVANS, WILLMOTT, M.D.

    Medical Science of To-Day. Ex. crn. 8vo; 24 Illustrations, 5s. nett.

Seeley, Service & Co Limited

EVENTS OF OUR OWN TIMES

Crown 8vo. With Illustrations, 5s. each.

The War in the Crimea. By General Sir E. HAMLEY, K.C.B.

The Indian Mutiny. By Colonel MALLESON, C.S.I.

The Afghan Wars, 1839–42, and 1878–80. By ARCHIBALD FORBES.

The Refounding of the German Empire. By Colonel MALLESON, C.S.I.

The Liberation of Italy. By the Countess MARTINENGO CESARESCO.

Great Britain in Modern Africa. By EDGAR SANDERSON, M.A.

The War in the Peninsula. By A. INNES SHAND.

FLETCHER, W. Y.
Bookbinding in France. Coloured Plates. Super-royal, sewed, 2s. 6d. nett ; half-linen, 3s. 6d. nett.

FORBES, ARCHIBALD.
The Afghan Wars of 1839–1842 and 1878–1880. With Four Portraits on Copper, and Maps and Plans. Crown 8vo, 5s.

FRASER, Sir ANDREW H. L.
Among Indian Rajahs and Ryots. With 34 Illustrations and a Map. Demy 8vo, 18s. nett. Third and Cheaper Edition, 5s. nett.

FRASER, DONALD.
Winning a Primitive People. Illustrated. Extra crown 8vo, 5s. nett.

FRIPP, Sir ALFRED D., K.C.V.O., & R. THOMPSON, F.R.C.S.
Human Anatomy for Art Students. Profusely Illustrated with Photographs and Drawings by INNES FRIPP, A.R.C.A. Square extra crown 8vo, 7s. 6d. nett.

FROBENIUS, LEO.
The Childhood of Man. A Popular Account of the Lives and Thoughts of Primitive Races. Translated by Prof. A. H. KEANE, LL.D. With 416 Illustrations. Demy 8vo, 16s. nett.

FRY, ROGER.
Discourses Delivered to the Students of the Royal Academy by Sir Joshua Reynolds. With an Introduction and Notes by ROGER FRY. With Thirty-three Illustrations. Square Crown 8vo 7s. 6d. nett.

GARDNER, J. STARKIE.
Armour in England. With Eight Coloured Plates and many other Illustrations. Super-royal 8vo, sewed, 3s. 6d. nett.

Foreign Armour in England. With Eight Coloured Plates and many other Illustrations. Super-royal 8vo, sewed, 3s. 6d. nett.

Armour in England. With Sixteen Coloured Plates and many other Illustrations. The two parts in one volume. Super-royal 8vo, cloth, gilt top, 9s. nett.

GARNETT, R., LL.D.
Richmond on Thames. Illustrated. Super-royal 8vo, sewed, 3s. 6d. nett.

GIBERNE, AGNES.
Beside the Waters of Comfort. Crown 8vo, 3s. 6d.

GIBSON, CHARLES R., F.R.S.E.
Electricity of To-Day. Its Works and Mysteries described in non-technical language. With 30 Illustrations. Extra crown 8vo, 5s. nett.

Scientific Ideas of To-day. A Popular Account in non-technical language of the Nature of Matter, Electricity, Light, Heat, &c., &c. With 25 Illustrations. Extra crown 8vo, 5s. nett.

How Telegraphs and Telephones Work. With many Illustrations. Crown 8vo, 1s. 6d. nett.

The Autobiography of an Electron. With 8 Illustrations. Long 8vo, 3s. 6d. nett.

Wireless Telegraphy. With many Illustrations. Ex. crn. 8vo, 2s. nett.

6

Seeley, Service & Co Limited

GODLEY, A. D.
Socrates and Athenian Society in his Day. Crown 8vo, 4s. 6d.
Aspects of Modern Oxford. With many Illustrations. Crown 8vo,
cloth, 2s. nett; lambskin, 3s. nett; velvet leather, in box, 5s. nett.

GOLDEN RECITER. (*See* James, Prof. Cairns.)

GOMES, EDWIN H., M.A.
Seventeen Years among the Sea Dyaks of Borneo. With 40 Illustrations and a Map. Demy 8vo, 16s. nett.

GRAHAME, GEORGE.
Claude Lorrain. Illustrated. Super-royal 8vo, 2s. 6d. nett; half-linen, 3s. 6d. nett.

GREGORY, Professor J. W., F.R.S., D.Sc.
Geology of To-Day. With 40 Illustrations and Diagrams. Ex. crn. 8vo, 5s. nett.

GRIFFITH, M. E. HUME.
Behind the Veil in Persia and Turkish Arabia. An Account of an Englishwoman's Eight Years' Residence amongst the Women of the East. With 37 Illustrations and a Map. Demy 8vo, 16s. nett.

GRINDON, LEO.
Lancashire. Brief Historical and Descriptive Notes. With many Illustrations. Crown 8vo, 6s.

GRUBB, W. BARBROOKE (Pioneer and Explorer of the Chaco).
An Unknown People in an Unknown Land. With Sixty Illustrations and a Map. Demy 8vo, 16s. nett. Third and Cheaper Edition, 5s. nett.
A Church in the Wilds. Illustrated. Extra crown 8vo, 5s. nett.

HADOW, W. H.
A Croatian Composer. Notes toward the Study of Joseph Haydn. Crown 8vo, 2s. 6d. nett.
Studies in Modern Music. First Series. Berlioz, Schumann, Wagner. With an Essay on Music and Musical Criticism. With Five Portraits. Crown 8vo, 7s. 6d.
Studies in Modern Music. Second Series. Chopin, Dvoràk, Brahms. With an Essay on Musical Form. With Four Portraits. Crown 8vo, 7s. 6d.

HAMERTON, P. G.
The Etchings of Rembrandt, and Dutch Etchers of the Seventeenth Century. By P. G. Hamerton and Laurence Binyon. With Eight Copper Plates and many other Illustrations. Super-royal 8vo, 7s. 6d. nett.
The Mount. Narrative of a Visit to the Site of a Gaulish City on Mount Beuvray. With a Description of the neighbouring City of Autun. Crown 8vo, 3s. 6d.
Round my House. Notes on Rural Life in Peace and War. Crown 8vo, with Illustrations, 2s. 6d. nett. Cheaper edition, 2s. nett.
Paris. Illustrated. New edition. Cloth, 2s. nett; leather, 3s. nett in special leather, full gilt, in box, 5s. nett.

HAMLEY, Gen. Sir E.
The War in the Crimea. With Copper Plates and other Illus. 5s.

HANOUM ZEYNEB (Heroine of Pierre Loti's Novel "Les Désenchantées.")
A Turkish Woman's European Impressions. Edited by Grace Ellison. With a portrait by Auguste Rodin and 23 other Illustrations from photographs. Crown 8vo, 6s. nett.

HARTLEY, C. GASQUOINE.
Things Seen in Spain. With Fifty Illustrations. Cloth, 2s. nett; leather, 3s. nett; velvet leather in a box, 5s. nett.

HAYWOOD, Capt. A. H. W.
Through Timbuctu & Across the Great Sahara. Demy 8vo, with 41 Illustrations and a Map. 16s. nett.

HENDERSON, Major PERCY E.
A British Officer in the Balkans. Through Dalmatia, Montenegro, Turkey in Austria, Magyarland, Bosnia and Herzegovina. With 50 Illustrations and a Map. Gilt top. Demy 8vo, 16s. nett.

Seeley, Service & Co Limited

HERBERT, GEORGE.

The Temple. Sacred Poems and Ejaculations. The Text reprinted from the First Edition. With Seventy-six Illustrations after ALBERT DÜRER, HOLBEIN, and other Masters. Crown 8vo, cloth, 2s. nett ; leather, 3s. nett. ; velvet leather in box, 5s. nett.

HOLLAND, CLIVE.

Things Seen in Japan. With Fifty beautiful illustrations of Japanese life in Town and Country. Small 4to, cloth, 2s. nett ; leather, 3s. nett ; velvet leather, in box, 5s. nett.

HUTCHINSON, Rev. H. N.

The Story of the Hills. A Popular Account of Mountains and How They were Made. With many Illustrations. Crown 8vo, 5s.

HUTTON, C. A.

Greek Terracotta Statuettes. With a Preface by A. S. MURRAY, LL.D. With Seventeen Examples printed in Colour and Thirty-six printed in Monochrome. 5s. nett ; or cloth, 7s. nett.

HUTTON, SAMUEL KING, M.B.

Among the Eskimos of Labrador. Demy 8vo ; with Forty-seven Illustrations and a Map. 16s. nett.

JAMES, CAIRNS.

The Golden Reciter. With an Introduction by CAIRNS JAMES, Professor of Elocution at the Royal Academy of Music, &c. With Selections from Rudyard Kipling, Thomas Hardy, R. L. Stevenson, Seton Merriman, H. G. Wells, Christina Rossetti, Anthony Hope, Austin Dobson, Maurice Hewlett, Conan Doyle, &c. &c. Extra crown 8vo, 704 pp. Cloth, 3s. 6d., and thin paper edition in cloth with gilt edges, 5s. "A more admirable book of its kind could not well be desired."
Liverpool Courier.

The Golden Humorous Reciter. Edited, and with a Practical Introduction, by CAIRNS JAMES, Professor of Elocution at the Royal College of Music and the Guildhall School of Music. A volume of Recitations and Readings selected from the writings of F. Anstey, J. M. Barrie, S. R. Crockett, Jerome K. Jerome, Barry Pain, A. W. Pinero, Owen Seaman, G. B. Shaw, &c. &c. Extra crown 8vo, over 700 pages, cloth, 3s. 6d. ; also a thin paper edition, with gilt edges, 5s.

THE ILLUMINATED SERIES

NEW BINDING.

Bound in antique leather with metal clasps. With illuminated frontispiece and title-page, and other illuminated pages. Finely printed at the Ballantyne Press, Edinburgh. Crown 8vo. Each copy in a box, 10s. 6d. nett. Also in real classic vellum. Each copy in a box. 10s. 6d. nett.

The Confessions of S. Augustine.
Of the Imitation of Christ. By THOMAS À KEMPIS.
The Sacred Seasons. By the BISHOP OF DURHAM. Also cloth, 6s. and 7s. 6d. nett.

JOY, BEDFORD.

A Synopsis of Roman History. Crown 8vo, 2s.

KEANE, Prof. A. H. (*See* FROBENIUS.)

LANG, ANDREW.

Oxford. New Edition. With 50 Illustrations by J. H. LORIMER, R.S.A., T. HAMILTON CRAWFORD, R.S.W., J. PENNELL, A. BRUNET-DEBAINES, A. TOUSSAINT, and R. KENT THOMAS. Extra crown 8vo, 2s. nett ; leather, 3s. nett. Special yapp leather, full gilt, in box, 5s. nett.
Ordinary Edition. Crown 4to. Printed by Messrs. T. & A. Constable of Edinburgh. 12s. 6d. nett.
Edition de Luxe, on unbleached Arnold hand-made paper, each copy numbered. Only 355 have been printed, of which 350 are for sale. Illustrated by GEORGE F. CARLINE, R.B.A. 25s. nett.

LEE, Sir SIDNEY.

Stratford-on-Avon. From the Earliest Times to the Death of Shakespeare. New revised edition, with additional Illustrations. Extra crown 8vo, 6s. Pocket Edition, 2s. nett ; leather, 3s. nett ; and in special yapp leather, full gilt, in box, 5s. nett.

Seeley, Service & Co Limited

LEFROY, W. CHAMBERS.
The Ruined Abbeys of Yorkshire. With many Illustrations by A.
BRUNET-DEBAINES and H. TOUSSAINT. Cr. 8vo, cloth, 2s. nett; leather, 3s. & 5s. nett.

LEYLAND, JOHN.
The Peak of Derbyshire. With Map, Etchings, and other Illustrations
by HERBERT RAILTON and ALFRED DAWSON. New Edition, Crown 8vo, cloth, 2s.;
leather, 3s.; velvet leather, in a box, 5s. nett.

LOFTIE, Rev. W. J.
The Inns of Court and Chancery. With many Illustrations, chiefly by
HERBERT RAILTON. Crown 8vo, cloth, 2s. nett; leather, 3s. nett and 5s. nett.
Westminster Abbey. With Seventy-four Illustrations, chiefly by HERBERT
RAILTON. Crown 8vo, 2s. 6d. Extra crown 8vo, 6s. and 7s. 6d.
Whitehall. With many Illustrations. Super-royal 8vo, sewed, 2s. 6d. nett;
half-linen, 3s. 6d. nett.

MACKENZIE, Rev. W. B.
Married Life and the Dwellings of the Righteous. 3s. 6d.

MALLESON, Colonel G. B., C.S.I.
The Indian Mutiny. With Copper Plates and other Illus. 5s.
The Refounding of the German Empire. With Portrait and Plans. 5s.

MINIATURE LIBRARY OF DEVOTION

Little Volumes of Short Extracts from the Christian Fathers. With Decorative
Title-page and Photogravure Frontispiece. 32mo, cloth extra, each 1s.
nett; leather, each 1s. 6d. nett. Also Three Volumes in leather in case,
4s. 6d. nett. White vellum with gilt edges, each volume in a box, 2s. nett.

1. Saint Augustine.
2. Jeremy Taylor.
3. Saint Chrysostom.
4. Bishop Andrewes.
5. John Keble.
6. Thomas à Kempis.
7. Canon Liddon.
8. Fénelon.
9. William Law.

MINIATURE PORTFOLIO MONO-GRAPHS

A New Edition in 16mo. Most of the Volumes have been carefully revised
by the Authors. Each Volume profusely Illustrated. Cloth, 2s. nett; leather, 3s.
nett; velvet leather, in box, 5s. nett.

Peter Paul Rubens. By R. A. M. STEVENSON.
Japanese Wood Engravings. By Professor W. ANDERSON.
Josiah Wedgwood. By Sir A. H. CHURCH, F.R.S., Professor of Chemistry,
Royal Academy of Arts. New & Revised Edition.
D. G. Rossetti. By F. G. STEPHENS, One of the Seven Members of the
Pre-Raphaelite Brotherhood.
The Early Work of Raphael. By JULIA CARTWRIGHT (Mrs. Ady).
Fair Women in Painting and Poetry. By WILLIAM SHARP (Fiona
Macleod).
Antoine Watteau. By CLAUDE PHILLIPS, Keeper of the Wallace
Collection.
Raphael in Rome. By JULIA CARTWRIGHT (Mrs. Ady).
The New Forest. By C. J. CORNISH, Author of "Life of the Zoo," &c.
The Isle of Wight. By C. J. CORNISH.
Gainsborough. By Sir WALTER ARMSTRONG, Keeper of the National
Gallery of Ireland.

9

Seeley, Service & Co Limited

THE LIBRARY OF MISSIONS

Illustrated. Extra Crown, 5s. 8vo, nett.

A Church in the Wilds. The Remarkable Story of the Establishment of the South American Mission amongst the hitherto Savage and Intractable Natives of the Paraguayan Chaco. By W. BARBROOKE GRUBB.

Winning a Primitive People. Sixteen Years' Work among the Warlike Tribe of the Ngoni and the Senga and Tumbuka Peoples of Central Africa. By the Rev. DONALD FRASER.

MITFORD, MARY RUSSELL.
Country Stories. With 68 Illustrations by GEORGE MORROW. Crown 8vo, cloth, gilt top, 2s. nett; also in leather, 3s. nett; and leather yapp, full gilt in box, 5s. nett.

MOULE, Archdeacon A. E.
New China and Old. Notes on the Country and People made during a Residence of Thirty Years. With Thirty Illustrations. New Edition, Revised. Crown 8vo, 5s.

MOULE, Right Rev. H. C. G., D.D. (Bishop of Durham).
The Sacred Seasons. Readings for the Sundays and Holy Days of the Christian Year. Printed in red and black throughout, and illuminated with specially drawn initial letters and ornaments, and with 12 illuminated pages printed in three colours and gold after illuminations in manuscripts at the British Museum. Extra crown 8vo, 6s. nett; also white cloth, in box, 7s. 6d. nett; antique leather with clasps, 10s. 6d. nett.
At the Holy Communion. Helps for Preparation and Reception. Cloth, 1s.; leather, 2s. nett; calf, 4s. 6d.
Christ's Witness to the Life to Come. Crown 8vo, 3s. 6d.
Grace and Godliness. Studies in the Epistle to the Ephesians. Crown 8vo, 2s. 6d.
In the House of the Pilgrimage. Hymns and Sacred Songs. 2s. 6d.
Imitations and Translations. Crown 8vo, 2s. 6d. nett.
Jesus and the Resurrection. Expository Studies on St. John xx. and xxi. Third Edition, 2s. 6d.
Lord's Supper, The. By BISHOP RIDLEY. Edited with Notes and a Life by the BISHOP OF DURHAM. Crown 8vo, 5s.
Our Prayer Book. Short Chapters on the Book of Common Prayer. 16mo, 1s.
Pledges of His Love, The. Thoughts on the Holy Communion. 16mo, 1s.
Prayers for the Home. A Month's Cycle of Morning and Evening Family Worship, with some Occasional Prayers. Crown 8vo, 3s. 6d.
Prayers and Promises. Messages from the Holy Scriptures. 16mo, 1s.
The Secret of the Presence, and other Sermons. Crown 8vo, 3s. 6d.
Temptation and Escape. Short Chapters for Beginners in the Christian Life. 16mo, 1s.
Thoughts on Christian Sanctity. 16mo, cloth, 1s.
Thoughts on Secret Prayer. 16mo, cloth, 1s.
Thoughts on the Spiritual Life. 16mo, cloth, 1s.
Thoughts on Union with Christ. 16mo, cloth, 1s.

MURRAY, A. S., LL.D.
Greek Bronzes. With Four Copper Plates and many other Illustrations. Super-royal 8vo, sewed, 3s. 6d. nett; cloth, 4s. 6d. nett.
Greek Bronzes, by Dr. MURRAY, and **Greek Terracotta Statuettes**, by C. A. HUTTON. With Four Photogravures, Eight Coloured Plates, and Seventy-seven other Illustrations. In one Volume. Super-royal 8vo, cloth, 10s. 6d. nett.

NETTLESHIP, J. T.
Morland, George. With Six Copper Plates and Thirty other Illustrations. Super-royal 8vo, sewed, 5s. nett; cloth, 6s. nett.

NEWTON, H., B.A.
In Far New Guinea. 47 Illus. and Map. 16s. nett.

Seeley, Service & Co Limited

THE NEW ART LIBRARY

EDITED BY M. H. SPIELMANN, F.S.A., & P. G. KONODY.

"The admirable New Art Library. . . . Thoroughly practical."—*The Connoisseur.*

THE ARTISTIC ANATOMY OF TREES.
By REX VICAT COLE. With hundreds of Illus. and Diagrams. Sq. ex. crn.
7s. 6d. nett.

THE PRACTICE AND SCIENCE OF DRAWING.
By HAROLD SPEED, Associé de la Société Nationale des Beaux-Arts ;
Member of the Society of Portrait Painters ; Professor of Drawing at the Goldsmiths'
College, &c. With Ninety-six Illustrations and Diagrams. Square ex. crn. 8vo, 6s. nett.

THE PRACTICE OF OIL PAINTING AND DRAWING.
By SOLOMON J. SOLOMON, R.A. With Eighty Illustrations. 6s. nett.

HUMAN ANATOMY FOR ART STUDENTS.
By Sir ALFRED DOWNING FRIPP, K.C.V.O., Lecturer upon Anatomy at
Guy's Hospital, London, and RALPH THOMPSON, Ch.M., F.R.C.S., with a chapter on
Comparative Anatomy, and Drawings by HARRY DIXON. With One hundred and fifty-
nine Photographs and Drawings. Square extra crown 8vo, 7s. 6d. nett.

MODELLING AND SCULPTURE.
By ALBERT TOFT, A.R.C.A., M.S.B.S. With 119 Photographs and
Drawings. Square extra crown 8vo, 6s. nett.

PAGE, J. Ll. WARDEN.
Exmoor, An Exploration of. With Maps, Etchings, and other Illustrations. Cheap Edition, 3s. 6d.

PENNELL, A. M., B.Sc.
Pennell of the Afghan Frontier. 20 Illustrations. 10s. 6d. nett.
"This book will interest many readers because it combines the fascinations of the ' Bible
in Spain,' Capt. Burton's ' Pilgrimages,' and ' Kim.' . . . It teems with adventure."—
Athenæum.

PENNELL, T. L., M.D., B.Sc., F.R.C.S.
Among the Wild Tribes of the Afghan Frontier. A Record of Six-
teen Years' Close Intercourse with the Natives of the Indian Marches. With an Intro-
duction by Field-Marshal LORD ROBERTS, V.C. Demy 8vo, 16s nett. Ex. crn. 8vo.
With 26 Illustrations and a Map. 5s. nett. Fourth and Cheaper Edition
Things Seen in Northern India. With 50 Illustrations. 2s., 3s., 5s. nett

PHILLIPS, CLAUDE.
The Earlier Work of Titian. With many Illustrations. Super-royal 8vo,
sewed, 3s. 6d. nett ; cloth, 4s. 6d. nett.
The Later Work of Titian. With many Illustrations. Super-royal 8vo,
sewed, 3s. 6d. nett ; cloth, 4s. 6d. nett.
Titian, a Study of his Life and Work. With Eight Copper Plates and
many other Illustrations. Super-royal 8vo, 9s. nett.
The Picture Gallery of Charles I. With many Illustrations. Super-
royal 8vo, sewed, 3s. 6d. nett ; cloth, 4s. nett
Frederick Walker. Sup.-roy. 8vo, sewed, 2s. 6d. nett ; half-linen, 3s. 6d. nett.
Antoine Watteau. Sup.-roy. 8vo, sewed, 2s. 6d. nett ; half-linen, 3s. 6d. nett ;
also small 4to, cloth, 2s. nett ; and 3s. and 5s. nett in leather.

POLLARD, A. W.
Italian Book Illustrations. Sewed, 2s. 6d. nett ; half-linen, 3s. 6d. nett.

PORTFOLIO MONOGRAPHS ON
ARTISTIC SUBJECTS

"A triumph of magnificent illustration and masterly editing."—*The Times.*

Many of the Volumes are issued in two forms and at various nett prices. Where two prices are
given, the first is that of the paper cover edition ; the second that of the cloth. When only
one price is given, the Volume is bound in paper only.

ANDERSON, Prof. W.
Japanese Wood Engravings. 2s. 6d. and 3s. 6d.

ARMSTRONG, Sir WALTER.
The Art of Velazquez. 3s. 6d.   The Life of Velazquez. 3s. 6d.
The Peel Collection and the Dutch School of Painting. 5s. and 7s.
Thomas Gainsborough. 3s. 6d.   W. Q. Orchardson. 2s. 6d. and 3s. 6d.

Seeley, Service & Co Limited

BEDFORD, W. K. R.
Malta. 2s. 6d.

BENHAM, Canon, and CHARLES WELCH, F.S.A.
Mediæval London. 3s. 6d., 5s., and 7s.
The Tower of London. 5s. and 7s.

BENHAM, Canon.
Old St. Paul's Cathedral. 5s. and 7s.

BINYON, LAURENCE.
Dutch Etchers of XVIIth Century. 2s. 6d. and 3s. 6d.
John Crome and J. S. Cotman. 3s. 6d.

BIRCH, G. H., F.S.A.
London on Thames. 5s. and 7s.

CARTWRIGHT, JULIA (Mrs. ADY).
Jules Bastien-Lepage. 2s. 6d. and 3s. 6d.
The Early Work of Raphael. 2s. 6d. and 3s. 6d.
Raphael in Rome. 2s. 6d. and 3s. 6d.

CHURCH, A. H., F.R.S.
Josiah Wedgwood. 5s. and 7s.

CORNISH, C. J.
The Isle of Wight. 2s. 6d. & 3s. 6d.   The New Forest. 2s. 6d. & 3s. 6d.

CUST, LIONEL, F.S.A.
The Engravings of Albert Dürer. 2s. 6d. and 3s. 6d.
The Paintings and Drawings of Albert Dürer. 3s. 6d.

DAVENPORT, CYRIL, F.S.A.
Royal English Bookbindings. 3s. 6d. & 4s. 6d.   Cameos. 5s. & 7s.

DAVIES, RANDALL, F.S.A.
English Society of the Eighteenth Century in Contemporary Art.

DESTRÉE, O. G.
The Renaissance of Sculpture in Belgium. 2s. 6d. and 3s. 6d.

FLETCHER, W. Y.
Bookbinding in France. 2s. 6d. and 3s. 6d.

GARDNER, J. STARKIE.
Armour in England. 3s. 6d.   Foreign Armour in England. 3s. 6d.

GARNETT, RICHARD, C.B., LL.D.
Richmond on Thames. 3s. 6d. and 4s. 6d.

GRAHAME, GEORGE.
Claude Lorrain. 2s. 6d. and 3s. 6d.

HAMERTON, P. G.
The Etchings of Rembrandt. 2s. 6d. and 3s. 6d.

HUTTON, C. A.
Greek Terracotta Statuettes. 5s. and 7s.

LOFTIE, W. J.
Whitehall. 2s. 6d. and 3s. 6d.

MURRAY, A. S., LL.D.
Greek Bronzes. 3s. 6d. and 4s. 6d.

Seeley, Service & Co Limited

NETTLESHIP, J. T.
George Morland. 5s. and 6s.

PHILLIPS, CLAUDE.
Frederick Walker. 2s. 6d. and 3s. 6d.
Antoine Watteau. 2s. 6d. and 3s. 6d.
The Picture Gallery of Charles I. 3s. 6d.
The Earlier Work of Titian. 3s. 6d.
The Later Work of Titian. 3s. 6d.

POLLARD, ALFRED W.
Italian Book Illustrations. 2s. 6d. and 3s. 6d.

PRIOR, E. S., F.S.A.
The Cathedral Builders in England. 5s. and 7s.

SHARP, WILLIAM.
Fair Women. 2s. 6d. and 3s. 6d.

STEPHENS, F. G.
Dante Gabriel Rossetti. 2s. 6d.

STEVENSON, R. A. M.
Peter Paul Rubens. 3s. 6d.

WAERN, CECILIA.
John La Farge. 3s. 6d.

WEALE, W. H. JAMES.
Gerard David, Painter and Illuminator. 2s. 6d. and 3s. 6d.

PRIOR, Canon E. S., F.S.A.
The Cathedral Builders of England. Illustrated. Super-royal 8vo, sewed, 5s. nett ; cloth, extra gilt top, 7s. nett.

QUILLER COUCH, SIR A. T.
The Pilgrims' Way. A Little Scrip for Travellers. In Prose and Verse. With end papers in colour, and gilt top. Fcap. 8vo, cloth, 3s. 6d. nett ; on thin paper, leather, 5s. nett. Buff leather yapp, in a box, 5s. nett.

RAGG, LONSDALE, B.D. (Oxon.), and L. M. RAGG.
Things Seen in Venice. With Fifty Illustrations. 2s., 3s., 5s. nett.

RANNIE, DOUGLAS (late Government Agent for Queensland.)
My Adventures Among South Sea Cannibals. Demy 8vo. With Thirty-nine Illustrations and a Map, 16s. nett.

RAWLING, Captain C. G.
The Land of the New Guinea Pygmies. Demy 8vo. With Forty-eight Illustrations and a Map, 16s. nett.

REYNOLDS, Sir JOSHUA.
Discourses Delivered to the Students of the Royal Academy. With an Introduction and Notes by ROGER FRY. With Thirty-Three Illustrations. Square extra Crown 8vo, 7s. 6d. nett.

ROCHE, C. E.
Things Seen in Holland. With Fifty Illustrations. Small 4to, cloth, 2s. nett ; lambskin, 3s. nett ; velvet leather, 5s. nett.

ROPES, A. R.
Lady Mary Wortley Montagu. With 8 Illustrations. Crown 8vo, cloth, 2s. 6d. nett.

RUSSELL, W. CLARK.
The British Seas. With upwards of Fifty Illustrations. Crown 8vo, cloth, 2s. ; leather, 3s. ; special yapp leather in box, 5s. nett.

SANDBY, W.
Thomas and Paul Sandby, Royal Academicians. Their Lives and Works. With many Illustrations. Crown 8vo, 7s. 6d.

Seeley Service & Co Limited

SANDERSON, E.
Great Britain in Modern Africa. With Four Portraits on Copper and
a Map. Crown 8vo, 5s.
SCOTT-ELLIOT, Professor G. F., M.A., B.Sc.
Botany of To-day. With Twenty-seven Illustrations. Ex. cr. 8vo, 5s. nett.
Prehistoric Man and His Story. With 70 Illustrations and Diagrams.
Demy 8vo, 7s. 6d. nett.

SCIENCE OF TO-DAY SERIES

The volumes of this series give an attractive, lucid, yet at the same time
scientifically accurate account of various subjects in non-technical language.
Large crown 8vo, 5s. nett.

Geology of To-Day. By Professor J. W. GREGORY, F.R.S., D.Sc.,
Professor of Geology at the University of Glasgow.
Submarine Engineering of To-day. By CHARLES W. DOMVILLE-FIFE.
Photography of To-day. By H. CHAPMAN JONES, F.I.C., F.C.S., F.R.P.S.
Aerial Navigation of To-day. By CHARLES C. TURNER.
Astronomy of To-Day. By C. G. DOLMAGE, M.A., LL.D., D.C.L., F.R.A.S.
Botany of To-day. By Prof. G. F. SCOTT-ELLIOT, M.A., B.Sc.
Electricity of To-Day. By CHARLES R. GIBSON, F.R.S.E.
Engineering of To-day. By THOMAS W. CORBIN.
Mechanical Inventions of To-Day. By T. W. CORBIN.
Medical Science of To-Day. By WILLMOTT EVANS, M.D.
Scientific Ideas of To-Day. By CHARLES R. GIBSON, F.R.S.E.

SEELEY'S ILLUSTRATED POCKET LIBRARY

Crown 8vo, cloth, gilt edge, 2s. nett; also in leather, 3s. nett; and
yapp leather in box at 5s. nett.

ADDISON and STEELE.
The Spectator in London. With Fifty-six Illustrations by RALPH
CLEAVER, and Headpieces by W. A. ATKIN BERRY, CLOUGH BROMLEY, &c.
CLARK, J. W., Registrary of the University of Cambridge.
Cambridge. With many Illustrations.
GODLEY, A. D.
Aspects of Modern Oxford. With many Illustrations.
HAMERTON, P. G.
Paris. With many Illustrations.
LEE, Sir SIDNEY.
Stratford-on-Avon. From the Earliest Times to the Death of Shake
speare. With 52 Illustrations by HERBERT RAILTON and E. HULL.
MITFORD, MARY RUSSELL.
Country Stories. With 68 Illustrations by GEORGE MORROW.
HERBERT, GEORGE.
The Temple. Sacred Poems and Ejaculations. The Text reprinted from
the first edition. With 76 Illustrations after DÜRER, HOLBEIN, and other Masters
LANG, ANDREW.
Oxford. With 40 Illustrations by various artists.
LEFROY, W. CHAMBERS.
The Ruined Abbeys of Yorkshire. With many Illustrations.
LEYLAND, JOHN.
The Peak of Derbyshire : its Scenery and Antiquities.
LOFTIE, W. J.
The Inns of Court. With 60 Illustrations.

Seeley, Service & Co Limited

RUSSELL, W. CLARK.
British Seas. With 50 Illustrations by J. C. HOOK, R.A., HAMILTON MACCALLUM, COLIN HUNTER, &c.

STEVENSON, R. L. Edinburgh. With many Illustrations by T. HAMILTON CRAWFORD, R.S.A. (This volume is only to be had in this series in leather, 5s. nett. For other editions of this book, see next page.)

SOLOMON, SOLOMON J., R.A.
The Practice of Oil Painting and Drawing. With 80 Illustrations. 6s. nett.

SPEED, HAROLD.
The Practice and Science of Drawing. With Ninety-six Illustrations and Diagrams. Square extra crown 8vo, 6s.

THE STANDARD LIBRARY
Extra Crown 8vo, With many Illustrations. Price 2s. 6d. nett.

Lady Mary Wortley Montagu. By A. R. ROPES.
Mrs. Thrale. By L. B. SEELEY.
Round My House. By P. G. HAMERTON.
Fanny Burney & Her Friends. By L. B. SEELEY.

STORY SERIES, THE. Extra crown 8vo, 5s. nett.
The Post Office and its Story. By EDWARD BENNETT. With 31 Illus.
Family Names and their Story. By the Rev. S. BARING GOULD.
The Press and its Story. By JAMES D. SYMON.
Prehistoric Man and His Story. By Professor G. F. SCOTT ELLIOT, M.A., B.Sc. With 70 Illustrations and Diagrams. Demy 8vo, 7s. 6d. nett.

SEELEY, Sir J. R.
Goethe Reviewed after Sixty Years. With Portrait. Crown 8vo, 3s. 6d.
A Short History of Napoleon the First. With Portrait. Crown 8vo, 5s.

SEELEY, Sir J. R., and Dr. ABBOTT.
English Lessons for English People. Crown 8vo, 4s. 6d.

SEELEY, L. B.
Mrs. Thrale, afterwards Mrs. Piozzi. With Eight Illustrations. Crown 8vo, 2s. 6d nett.
Fanny Burney and her Friends. With Eight Illustrations. Crown 8vo, 2s. 6d nett.

SHAND, A. INNES.
The War in the Peninsula. With Portraits and Plans. 5s.

SHARP, WILLIAM.
Fair Women. Illustrated. Super-royal 8vo, sewed, 2s. 6d. nett; half-linen, 3s. 6d. nett. Also new edition, small 4to, cloth, 2s. nett; leather, 3s. and 5s. nett.

STEPHENS, F. G.
Rossetti, D. G. Super-royal 8vo, sewed, 2s. 6d. nett; also small 4to, cloth, 2s. nett; leather, 3s. nett; velvet leather, in a box, 5s. nett.

STEVENSON, R. L.
Edinburgh. Fcap. 8vo, with Frontispiece, gilt top, cloth, 2s. nett; leather, 3s. nett. Crown 8vo, Illustrated, cloth, 3s. 6d. Library Edition. Crown 8vo, buckram, dark blue, gilt top, Sixteen Full-page Illustrations, 6s. Presentation Edition. Extra crown 8vo, with Sixty-four Illustrations, 6s.; also People's Edition, demy 8vo, 6d. nett; cloth, 1s. With Twenty-four Illustrations in colour, by JAMES HERON. Crown 4to. Printed by Messrs. T. & A. Constable, of Edinburgh. Ordinary Edition, 12s. 6d. nett. EDITION DE LUXE, limited to 385 copies, of which only 375 are for sale, printed on unbleached Arnold handmade paper, and bound in buckram, with paper label, each copy numbered, 25s. nett. With 12 Coloured Illustrations by JAMES HERON. Pott 4to, 6s. nett.

15

Seeley, Service & Co Limited

STEVENSON, R. A. M.
Rubens, Peter Paul. Illustrated. Super-royal 8vo, 3s. 6d. nett, sewed. Also small 4to, cloth, 2s. nett; leather, 3s. nett and 5s. nett.

STIGAND, Captain C. H., F.R.G.S., F.Z.S.
To Abyssinia Through an Unknown Land. With Thirty-six Illustrations and Two Maps. Demy 8vo, 16s. nett.

SWANN, ALFRED J.
Fighting the Slave Hunters in Central Africa. With Forty-five Illustrations and a Map. Demy 8vo, 16s. nett. Extra crown 8vo, 5s. nett.

TALBOT, F. A.
The Makings of a Great Canadian Railway. Demy 8vo. With Forty-one Illustrations and a Map. 16s. nett.

THE THINGS SEEN SERIES

Each volume with 50 Illustrations. Small 4to, cloth, 2s. nett; leather, 3s. nett; and velvet leather, in a box, 5s. nett.

Things Seen in Sweden. By W. BARNES STEVENI.
Things Seen in Oxford. By N. J. DAVIDSON, B.A. (Oxon.)
Things Seen in Russia. By W. BARNES STEVENI.
Things Seen in Palestine. By A. GOODRICH FREER.
Things Seen in Japan. By CLIVE HOLLAND.
Things Seen in China. By J. R. CHITTY.
Things Seen in Egypt. By E. L. BUTCHER.
Things Seen in Holland. By C. E. ROCHE.
Things Seen in Spain. By C. GASQUOINE HARTLEY.
Things Seen in Northern India. By T. L. PENNELL, M.D. B.Sc.
Things Seen in Venice. By LONSDALE RAGG, B.D. (Oxon.)

TOFT, ALBERT, Hon., A.R.C.A., M.S.B.S.
Modelling and Sculpture. Profusely Illustrated with 119 Photographs and Drawings. Square extra crown 8vo, 6s. nett.

TORDAY, E.
Camp and Tramp in African Wilds. Demy 8vo. With Forty-five Illustrations and a Map, 16s. nett.

TOWNSHEND, Captain A. T.
A Military Consul in Turkey. With 29 Illustrations. Demy 8vo, 16s. nett.

TREMEARNE, Major A. J. N.
The Tailed Head-Hunters of Nigeria. Demy 8vo, with 38 Illustrations and a Map. 16s. nett.

TURNER, CHARLES C.
Aerial Navigation of To-day. With Seventy Illustrations and Diagrams. Extra crown 8vo, 5s. nett.

WAERN, C.
John La Farge. Illustrated. Super-royal 8vo, sewed, 3s. 6d. nett.

WEALE, W. H. JAMES.
Gerard David, Painter and Illuminator. Illustrated. Super-royal 8vo, sewed, 2s. 6d. nett; half-linen, 3s. 6d. nett.

WEEKS, JOHN H.
Among Congo Cannibals. Demy 8vo. With Fifty-four Illustrations and a Map, 16s. nett.
Among the Primitive Bakongo. 40 Illus. and Map. 16s. nett.

WELCH, C., and Canon BENHAM.
Mediæval London. With a Frontispiece in Photogravure, Four Plates in Colour, and many other Illustrations. Super-royal 8vo, sewed, 5s. nett; cloth, gilt top 7s. nett. Also extra crown 8vo, 3s. 6d. nett

WICKS, MARK.
To Mars via the Moon. An Astronomical Story. With Sixteen Illustrations and Diagrams. Extra crown 8vo, 5s

WILLIAMSON, R. W., M.Sc.
The Ways of the South Sea Savage. 43 Illustrations. 16s. nett.

www.ingramcontent.com/pod-product-compliance
Lightning Source LLC
Chambersburg PA
CBHW062034090426
42740CB00016B/2906